I0867225

US Marine Raiders' and Paramarines' Kitbag

US Marine Raiders' and Paramarines' Kitbag

Uniforms and Equipment of the US Marine Corps' Elite Units in WWII

Jim Moran

Frontline Books

First published in Great Britain in 2025 by
Frontline Books
An imprint of Pen & Sword Books Limited
Yorkshire – Philadelphia

Copyright © Jim Moran 2025

ISBN 978 1 52677 817 8

The right of Jim Moran to be identified as
Author of this Work has been asserted by him in accordance
with the Copyright, Designs and Patents Act 1988.

A CIP catalogue record for this book is
available from the British Library.

All rights reserved. No part of this book may be reproduced, transmitted, downloaded, decompiled or reverse engineered in any form or by any means, electronic or mechanical including photocopying, recording or by any information storage and retrieval system, without permission from the Publisher in writing. No part of this book may be used or reproduced in any manner for the purpose of training artificial intelligence technologies or systems.

Typeset by Mac Style
Printed and bound in India by Replika Press Pvt. Ltd.

MIX
Paper | Supporting responsible forestry
FSC™ C016779

The Publisher's authorised representative in the EU for product safety is Authorised Rep Compliance Ltd., Ground Floor, 71 Lower Baggot Street, Dublin D02 P593, Ireland.
www.arccompliance.com

For a complete list of Pen & Sword titles please contact

PEN & SWORD BOOKS LIMITED
47 Church Street, Barnsley, South Yorkshire, S70 2AS, England
E-mail: enquiries@pen-and-sword.co.uk
Website: www.pen-and-sword.co.uk
or
PEN AND SWORD BOOKS
1950 Lawrence Road, Havertown, PA 19083, USA
E-mail: uspen-and-sword@casematepublishers.com
Website: www.penandswordbooks.com

CONTENTS

Raider Battalions

ACKNOWLEDGEMENTS

Numerous people have given generously of their time and expertise to assist me in producing this book. In particular, Susan Brubaker and Cara Newcomer at the US Marine Corps Historical Division in the Al Gray Centre, Quantico, Virginia. Thanks also to Owen Conner (Museum of the Marine Corps).

My thanks also to Major Rick Spooner USMC (Ret) for all his help and encouragement over many years, the Raider Hall at Quantico, in particular Lt Col Joe Shusko, Martial Arts Director USMC and Sergeant Johnson, who provided access to all their information and museum exhibits during my visit.

Special thanks go to Doug Bailey, Marine Corps veteran, friend of many years standing and collector par excellence without whose assistance this book would not have been possible. Doug's collection of Raider and Paramarine material is exceptional and has been a major source of information for me and indeed for many historians. We have talked for a long time about producing this book and his help and encouragement has been invaluable.

Semper Fidelis
Jim Moran

INTRODUCTION

PARAMARINES

The US Marine Parachute troops – known during World War Two as 'Paramarines' but later changed due to its modern connotation of 'something less than real' – began formation on 28 May 1941 with Company A. The 1st Parachute Battalion did not complete formation until 28 March 1942.

Four battalions were eventually formed, of which only the first three were operational by the time these units were disbanded in January/February 1944. The paratroopers (grouped as 1st Parachute Regiment in April 1943) first saw action in the Guadalcanal and Tulagi fighting in August 1942 (1st Battalion). Although the only combat jump by Marines was, ironically, to be in southern France as part of an OSS unit, two unit combat jumps in the Pacific – at Kolombangara and Kavieng – were in fact planned but subsequently cancelled. The Paramarines served with distrinction as infantry throughout the Solomons campaign.

Despite the fact that they were eventually committed to action as infantry, the Paramarines were issued, during their brief existence, with at least three distinct patterns of jump smock, apparently worn only during training in the United States. They were also issued with further bespoke items of equipment in addition to the basic Marine Corps 782 gear.

CHAPTER 1

PARACHUTIST UNIFORMS

The **Coverall, Parachutist, HBT, Sage Green,** first appeared before the entry of the United States into the war, being designed during 1941. The design is credited to Capt. Robert H Williams, who drew upon photographs of German Fallschirmjäger troops taken after the fall of Ében Émael, Belgium, on 10 May 1940. From the outset, it was believed that the paratroopers would need specially designed clothing and rather than the two-piece uniform developed for the US Army Airborne, the US Marine Corps favoured a step-in type of smock similar to the German Fallschirmjäger issue.

The first smock was originally intended to be worn with the standard issue wool shirt and trousers, but was later worn over the adopted one-piece HBT mechanics' coverall 'borrowed' from Marine armoured troops. Made of plain sage green HBT fabric, it had short integral legs reaching to mid-thigh and a front fastening by means of a full length throat to crotch zipper. The back was 'bi-swing' design with vertical pleats each side. The sleeves had cuff bands, adjusted and fastened by a single bronze US Marine Corps button. The elbows and upper forearms were protected by large external cushion pads made of horsehair, covered with tan canvas and stitched to the sleeves in a criss-cross pattern.

On each side of the lower part of the smock, extending from the hip to the lower thigh, was a large pocket made of tan canvas, the rounded lower edge extending below the edge of the legs. These were closed at the top with horizontal zippers (though an earlier variant had top flaps fastened by two black glove snaps). The lower cargo pockets are believed to have had removable horsehair inserts, worn during the jump to protect the hips on landing and removable afterwards to enable the pockets to be used to carry equipment. Later examples show the left hand lower pocket having an external rectangular vertical pouch, enclosed with a top flap and single black glove snap. This pocket is thought to have been for the Western Cutlery paratrooper knife or an immediate-use magazine for the M55 Reising SMG.

The smock also had two further front and one rear external upper pockets, the front right hand pocket measuring 6 ½ by 7 inches, with bellows pleats at the front and secured by a square top flap and three plain black glove snaps. The left hand side pocket was smaller, 6 by 3½ inches, with side bellows to allow expansion and a square-cut top flap with two black glove snaps. The Marine Corps eagle, globe and anchor above 'USMC' lettering was stencilled in black on the left side above the chest pocket, the lettering often being applied to the pocket flap itself. It is uncertain if these chest pockets were intended for specific contents, but it is possible that the left hand one was designed to hold two first aid dressings and the right hand one K rations.

The pocket on the upper rear of the smock is unusual. It may have been intended simply as a cargo pocket or a pouch for the poncho, which does fit when folded. This pocket measures 10 x 8 inches and is sewn on externally, it has side bellows to allow expansion and a square top flap fastening which measures 10 by 4 inches, secured with three plain black glove snaps.

This smock was also produced (at least in prototype) in reversible camouflage fabric, but the design proved too complex for wartime production, thus initiating development of a new, specific, camouflage jump smock.

Coverall, Parachutist, Camouflage

During late 1942 or early in 1943, with the onset of the use of camouflage clothing by other specialist units, the plain sage green 'coverall, parachutist, HBT', used in the initial training stages since 1941, was dropped in favour of a camouflage version. The 'coverall, parachutist, HBT, camouflage,' designed by Lt Col Marcellis J Howard and Capt Harry L Torgerson as part of a 3-piece combat jump suit, appears from the photographic record to have been used mainly – or even perhaps exclusively – for Stateside training. No photographic evidence has been found by the author of these smocks being worn in combat in the Pacific.

The second pattern jump smock (or first pattern camouflage jump smock) was again a step-in design like the initial sage green pattern. It was intended to be worn with the 'uniform, utility, HBT, camouflage (parachutist)'. The smock was reversible, in the familiar greens and browns pattern, the 'green' side normally worn outermost. It retained the horsehair impact pads on the elbows as used on the first uncamouflaged pattern smock but these were now sewn internally with no external criss-cross stitching. There was no cuff adjustment on the sleeves, which were now fastened with a single glove snap. The full length front closure was six plain black glove snaps spaced between throat and crotch. In the front of the two short integral legs were two large pockets positioned across the full width of the leg. The horizontal slash openings, giving through access to the trouser pockets beneath, were covered by large pointed flaps fastened by three glove snaps. An upper pair of pockets, again internally hung, were positioned on either side of the chest. These aligned with the pockets of the camouflage shirt/jacket intended to be worn under the smock, access being through slash openings set at 30 degrees to the vertical and angled upwards and outwards. Each was covered by a pointed flap, again fastened by three glove snaps. Documentary records suggest that the chest pocket layout of the first, uncamouflaged, smock proved inconvenient due to the position of the chest-mounted reserve parachute pack which made the pockets inaccessible.

On the rear of the smock was a large, internal cargo pocket, placed centrally. This was accessed from both left and right, with a zip fastened opening at each. The opening was 10 inches long, set at an angle of 50 degrees to the vertical, angled upwards and inwards and covered by a pointed flap fastened by three black glove snaps.

Coverall, Parachutist, Camouflage (modified)

The complex pocket design of the second pattern jump smock made it costly to produce and it was soon decided to simplify the detail. The 'coverall, parachutist, HBT, camouflage (modified)' appeared in the summer or early autumn of 1943 and was of the same basic outline as the previous model. Still a step-in smock, it retained the reversible camouflage pattern in greens and browns and the front fastening of six plain black glove snaps positioned as previously. The elbow pads were sewn to the outside of the sleeves with a criss-cross pattern, the horsehair pad being covered with camouflage fabric.

The pocket layout on the chest of the smock resembled that of the second pattern USMC two-piece camouflage utilities. It is thought – although there is no substantiating evidence for or against – that the second pattern two=piece camouflage utilities, P1944, were in fact originally intended to be worn with this third pattern camouflage smock, making the whole ensemble a replacement for the earlier second pattern smock and two-piece 'utility uniform, HBT, camouflage (parachutist)'. However, with the disbanding of the parachute units it would appear that the two-piece uniform was incorporated into the basic Marine infantryman's issue, the smocks being cut down and re-emerging as utility shirts (sometimes referred to as the 'fourth pattern jump smock').

The third pattern jump smock had four internally hung pockets, two at chest level and two at waist level. Access to all four was by vertical slash openings, set closely on each side of the smock's front closure, the top pair between the level of the second and fourth glove snaps, the lower pair between the fourth and sixth. Each opening was secured by a central black glove snap, these being placed just above the third and just below the fifth front closure fasteners.

A large internal cargo pocket ran the full width of the rear of the smock from left to right seam. Access was by vertical openings set in each seam, secured by 10-inch zip fasteners and covered by vertical rectangular flaps, each fastened by three black glove snaps.

Again, evidence of the use of this pattern of smock for any purpose other than training and exercises is lacking

Uniform, Utility, HBT, Camouflage (Parachutist)

This suit, part of the 3-piece camouflage combat/jump suit, was designed and intended to be worn under the second pattern jump smock (first pattern camouflage) and as a utility/combat suit in its own right. The intention appears to have been for the jump smock to be discarded on the drop zone.

The uniform was originally made in canvas of shelter half weight, but subsequently in HBT fabric. The coat was a loose fitting reversible camouflage shirt/jacket, the front closure fastening with six plain black glove snaps and the cuffs having adjustable closure with a single glove snap. There were short vents in the bottom of each body side seam. The two breast pockets were internally hung so that when the jacket was worn 'brown' side out they appeared as bellows patch pockets. On both green and brown sides of the jacket the pockets were accessed through slash openings set at approximately 30 degrees to the vertical, angled upwards and outwards and covered by pointed flaps secured by a single central glove snap.

The trousers, again reversible, had plain bottoms and an exposed front fly fastened by five glove snaps. The waistband had belt loops on both green and brown sides and six metal eyelets, four at the front, two at the back, for attaching the webbing suspenders of the P1941 pack system. At the front of the hips were two internally hung pockets, accessed on the green side by slash openings set at 45 degrees outwards and downwards. When the trousers were worn brown side out these appeared as patch pockets with the openings covered by angled, pointed flaps fastened by three black glove snaps.

Across the rear of the trousers was a single cargo 'butt' pocket, which hung externally when worn green side out and internally when worn brown side out. Access from both sides was by two openings set at 45 degrees outwards and downwards. Each opening on both sides was covered by a pointed flap secured by three glove snaps.

The P1944 two-piece camouflage utility uniform design (see US Marine Corps Uniforms and Equipment in WW2 by this author) is in many respects very similar to, and mirrors the pocket layout of, the third pattern jump smock (second pattern camouflage) in the same way that these paratrooper utilities described above mirror the second pattern jump smock (first pattern camouflage). As already mentioned, this gives rise to speculation that each uniform was originally intended to be worn under a jump smock, but was too late to be adopted before the disbandment of the Paramarines.

Near Fredericksburg, Virginia, July 1941. Cpl Grover, 1st Parachute Bn, landed in a tree during Army/ Marine manoeuvres. He wears an early style of first pattern jump smock, note flaps on thigh pockets instead of zippers, also lack of elbow pads. The jump smock is worn over basic summer khaki trousers and white skivvy shirt. Note also lack of jump boots (NA 127 – N-504477)

Stateside c 1942. Paramarines being interviewed for CBS during parachute training All except instructors wear one-piece HBT coveralls and jump boots, along with the leather jump helmet which was a trademark of the Paramarines – either worn by itself as here, or under the M1 steel helmet. (via Doug Bailey)

Paramarines undergoing training May 1943. They are wearing 1-piece or 2-piece HBT utilities. Note 1st pattern jump boots and leather jump caps under their M1 helmets. Note also Western W31 drop knives in the back pocket of the two Paramarines left, also what appears to be the padded end cap of an equipment drop canister, front.

Paramarines training at Highstown, New Jersey. All wear 1-piece HBT coveralls and a mixture of wool and leather jump helmets. Note EGA and USMC in black on pocket stencil on coveralls, authorised in November 1941.

Paramarine demonstrates the correct way to exit the cargo plane. He wears 1-piece HBT coveralls with 1st pattern jump boots and has a TB dual purpose parachute.

Lakehurst, NJ. Corp Richard Tomkins, USMC, prepares to exit the transport plane on his graduation jump.

Paramarine demonstrates correct procedure for exiting a transport plane. He wears 1-piece HBT coveralls with 1st pattern jump boots. Note Reising M55 folding stock SMG on top of his reserve chute.

Paramarines practice correct landing procedure. All wear 1-piece HBT coveralls.

Parachute Graduates, Camp Gillespie. All wear two-piece HBT utilities with 1st pattern jump boots. Note white name tapes over left breast pocket, also leather jump helmets under M1 helmet liners.

Paramarines undergoing map reading training. All are wearing summer issue shirt and trousers with 1st pattern jump boots along with TB dual purpose parachutes.

A stick of Paramarines entrain a waiting R4D cargo plane. There were never enough planes to allow the mass drops in the Pacific, unlike Europe.

A stick of Paramarines pose for the camera prior to taking off for one of their required six jumps to qualify as Parachutists. All are wearing 1-piece HBT coveralls with 1st pattern jump boots, leather jump caps and TB dual purpose parachutes.

A group of Paramarines get final instructions from their training officer prior to take off. They all wear 1-piece HBT coveralls with 1st pattern jump boots and wool jump caps, also TB dual purpose parachutes.

Paramarines on board prior to jumping. All wear 1-piece HBT coveralls and wool jump caps, along with TB, DP parachutes.

Paramarine preparing for practice jump. He wears 2-piece HBT utilities. Note leather jump helmet under his M1 helmet, also Western W31 drop knife in his back pocket. (via Doug Bailey)

San Diego 1941. Paramarines prepare for a practice jump. All wear 1st pattern jump smocks over 1-piece HBT coveralls with 1st pattern jump boots and leather jump helmets under their M1 helmets. All have TB, DP parachutes and carry Reising M55 SMGs. (NA 127-N-402928)

Paramarines show off their newly issued Reising M55 SMGs. All are wearing 1st pattern jump smocks over one-piece HBT coveralls with highly polished 1st pattern jump boots.

Paramarines on board ready to take one of their required six jumps to qualify as Parachutists. They wear the 1st pattern jump smock over one-piece coveralls and a mixture of cloth and leather jump helmets.

San Diego, February 1943. PFC Kleist poses for the camera after a successful parachute drop. He wears 2nd pattern jump smock (1st pattern camouflage) over 2-piece camouflage utilities with 2nd pattern jump boots (extended boondockers) and wears leather jump helmet under his M1 helmet.

Iwo Jima, March 1945. Former Paramarine Ptn Sgt Jennings still wears his 2-piece Parachutist's camouflage utilities and 2nd pattern jump boots.

Quantico, Virginia 1941. Paramarines pose for Defence Department photographs, wearing the USMC one-piece HBT mechanic's coveralls and the original forest green wool jump helmet, later replaced by the leather jump helmet. Note M1928A1 Thompson with 50-round drum. (NA 127-N-529482)

Tarawa, November 1943. Although paratrooper jump smocks were worn almost exclusively during training in the USA, the Marine seen here inspecting Japanese gun positions after the fall of Betio/Tarawa wears a first pattern jump smock (probably cut down) as a field jacket, the rear cargo pocket showing clearly. (NA 127-N-64410)

Stateside 1942. Paramarine on the range with his Reising M50 sub-machine gun, standard issue (along with the M55 folding stock version) to Marine Parachute units. Unfortunately, the Reising did not stand up to combat conditions and was often ditched in favour of the Thompson. Note also fibre helmet with cap badge attached. (via Doug Bailey)

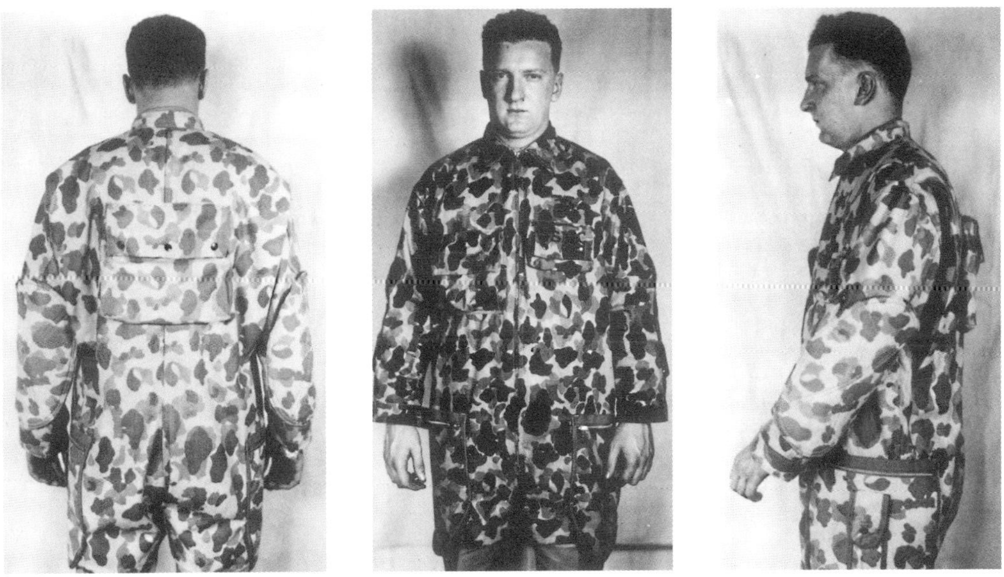

Washington DC, August 1942. With the decision by the Marine Parachute Units to adopt a specialist camouflage uniform, like the Marine Raiders, the first attempt at a camouflage jump smock was simply to produce the first pattern sage green jump smock in camouflage material. Unfortunately, to produce this in reversible brown and green camouflage with all the intricate pleats and pocket arrangements was an absolute tailor's nightmare, these photographs possibly showing the only example produced. This led to the design of the second pattern jump smock (or first pattern camouflage smock) in late 1942.

Tarawa, November 1943. Wounded Marines receive blood plasma at beach aid station. The Corpsman standing at centre wears the Paratrooper first aid kit. Note the white disc Corpsman identification on helmets, high on right shoulder of man bending lowest over litter and on rear trouser pocket of man in left foreground. (NA 127-N-63779)

San Diego, February 1943. Men of Co L, 3rd Parachute Bn, pose before going overseas. All wear jump smocks over camouflage utilities. Note camouflage and khaki drop bags for weapons strapped under reserve chutes. (via Doug Bailey)

Camp Elliot, February 1943. Members of 3rd Parachute Bn pose in a fine array of Paramarine uniforms and equipment. Most wear first pattern camouflage jump smocks; one (second left, front row) wears the Parachutist's two-piece camouflage utility suit. Note shoulder holster worn by battalion CO, Maj Vance, (front row, centre); also his Marine Corps map case on right hip, unlike the standard M1928 dispatch cases worn by two men on his left. Maj Torgerson (back row, extreme right) has his Johnson carbine slung. One man (second left, back row) wears the pale 'extended boondocker' jump boots and leather jump helmet. (NA 127-GC-248-35415)

Camp Kiser, New Caledonia, April 1943. The basic 'kit, first aid, paratrooper' which was standard issue to all Paramarine Corpsmen, is seen here worn by Dr Wendell White over the first pattern jump smock. White also appears to have some form of early helmet cover, probably of hessian or HBT material, as used by the Raiders. (NA 127-N-55045)

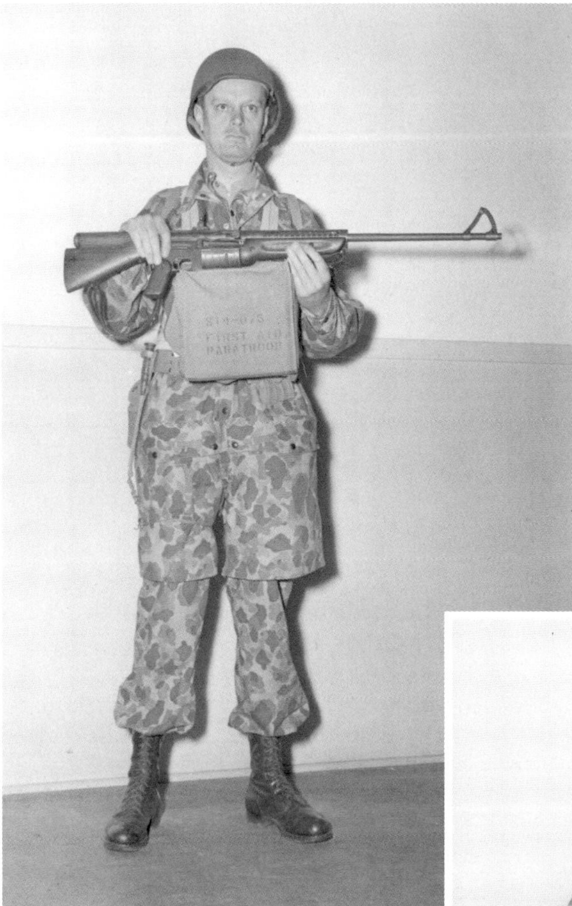

Camp Elliot, February 1943. Lt Leonard, USN, a Corpsman attached to the Paramarines, wears the Parachutist's two-piece camouflage utility uniform under a second pattern (first pattern camouflage) jump smock. Note S14 paratrooper first aid chest pack. Weapons are Marine Corps utility knife (K-bar) and a 'one off' carbine made for Maj Harry Torgerson, USMC, by his personal friend Melvin Johnson. Johnson supplied semi-automatic rifles and light machine guns to the Marine Corps and Torgerson's unique 'trademark' carbine was a cross between the two. (NA 127-N-35436)

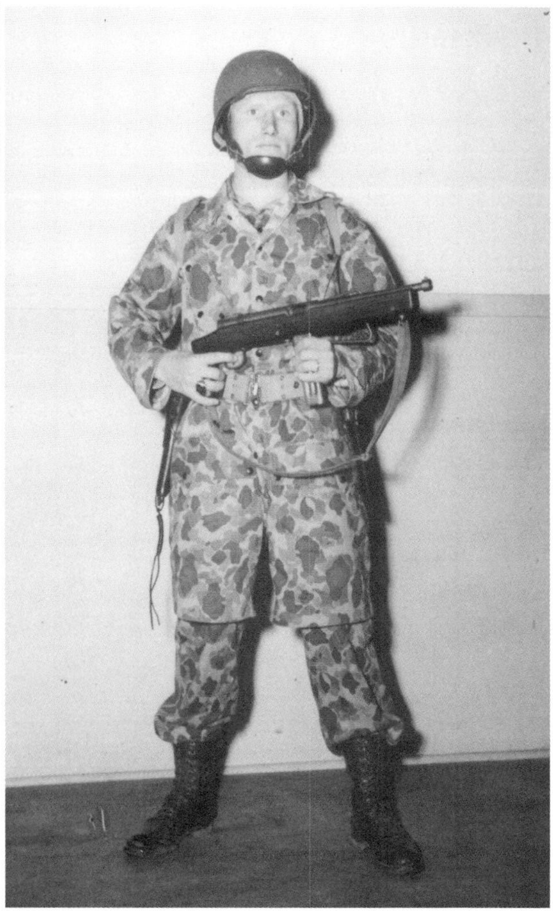

Camp Elliot, February 1943. 2nd Lt Gass models the (then) new Paramarine camouflage uniform. He wears the two-piece utility suit under the second pattern jump smock (first pattern camouflage) with the leather jump helmet under the standard M1 helmet. Boots are the initial Paramarine type without toe cap, later supplemented by Corcoran jump boots with toe caps and by the so-called 'extended boondockers'. Weapons are the 1911A1 .45 automatic pistol in leather hip holster and Reising M55 SMG. Gass also wears the Marine type musette bag as a field pack, note broad pads just visible on the shoulder straps. (NA 127-GC-248-35435)

New Caledonia, Spring 1943. Troopers of Co. L, 3rd Parachute Bn, display the uniform, utility, HBT, camouflage (parachutist). Note large slanting shirt pocket flaps fastened by a single glove snap, Johnson LMGs and M1A1 carbine and K-bars scabbarded on troopers' left hips. (via Doug Bailey)

Koiaris raid, Bougainville, November 1943. Men of 1st Parachute Bn fire a captured Japanese 37mm gun. Most wear two-piece parachutist's utilities; note revolver butt showing in left breast pocket of man at left with folding stock M1A1 carbine. The man at far right has a 'knuckle knife' (possibly Australian made) on his belt. (NA 127-N-69772)

Paramarine training on New Caledonia. Note 3rd pattern jump smocks (2nd pattern camouflage) with 2nd pattern jump boots. Weapons are Johnson LMG and Johnson rifle.

Bougainville, November 1943. Paramarines wade across typical terrain, all three wearing the special paratrooper two-piece camouflage utility suit. Note variety of entrenching shovels, pick-mattocks, wire cutters. The trooper in the centre has a camouflage shovel cover on his near hip. Left and centre men carry M1A1 folding stock carbines, the trooper with the Springfield rifle with rubber stock boot is probably a grenadier. (NA 127-N-68621)

New River, Carolina, October 1943. Paramarine wearing third pattern jump smock (second pattern camouflage) models the Navy MAB radio (note skullcap headset under helmet). The MAB was standard equipment for Paramarines and sometimes had a rigger-made camouflage carrying bag instead of the khaki one illustrated. The second pattern camouflage smock was the result of an attempt to simplify the complex pocket layout of its predecessor. Note characteristic front pockets and patch elbow pads. The smock is worn here, unusually, over forest green trousers and khaki shirt. (NA 127-GC-495-5885)

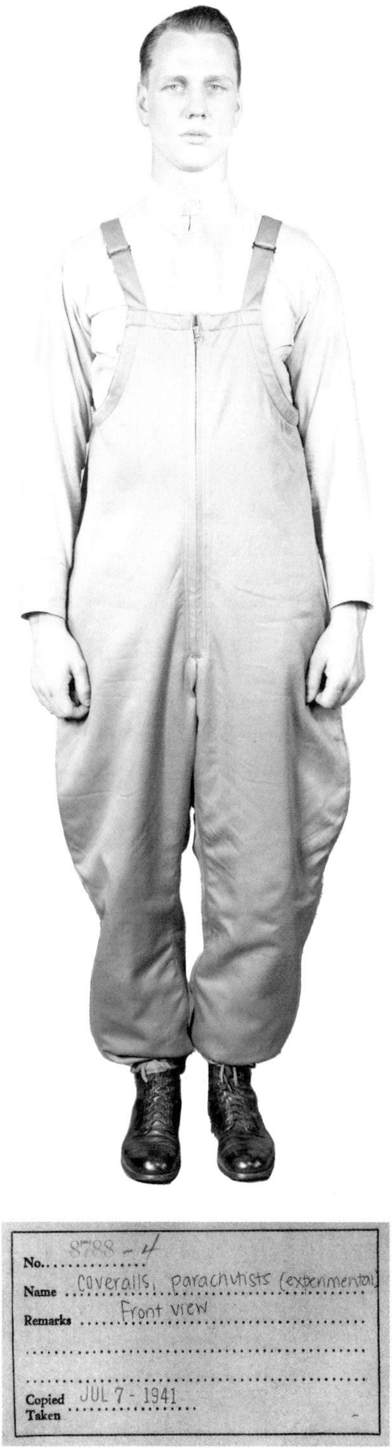

QM photographs of Coveralls, Parachutist (Experimental). Basically the Army's trousers, combat, winter, dated July 7, 1941. Dropped in favour of Capt Williams' jump smock design.

Bougainville 1943. Maj Harry Torgerson, 3rd Parachute Bn, receives a necktie for Christmas – a most useful gift for the jungle! Torgerson wears parachute jump wings on the left breast of his khaki shirt. Note also dungaree trousers, paratrooper boots and Torgerson's 'personal' Johnson carbine. (NA 127-N-68786)

QM photographs of Coveralls, Parachutist (Experimental) dated August 5, 1941. Designed by Capt Robert H Williams, USMC.

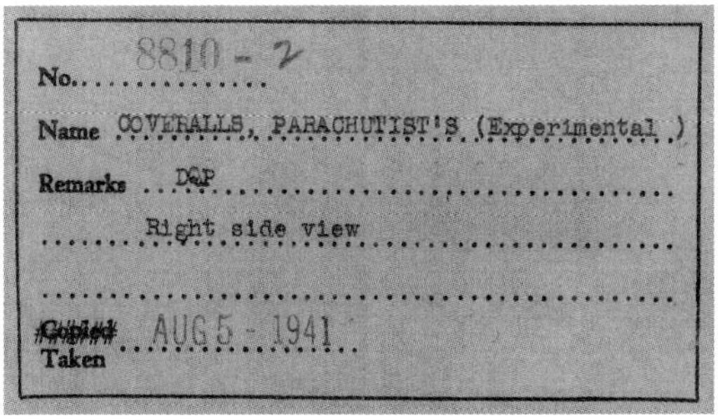

No. 8810 - 2
Name COVERALLS, PARACHUTIST'S (Experimental)
Remarks DQP
Right side view
Copied Taken AUG 5 - 1941

QM photograph of "Coveralls, Parachutist (Experimental)", right side view.

Coverall, mechanics, HBT, sage green, P1941: initially issued to armoured troops and later to Marine paratroops. Note steel US Marine Corps buttons. The eagle, globe and anchor USMC stencil was sometimes to be seen on the top left pocket, but was not authorised until November 1941. In the rear view, note the long wrench pocket below the right rear patch pocket.

Coveralls HBT, Mechanics. Note USMC and EGA in black on top left pocket.

First pattern jump smock, officially Coverall, Parachutist, HBT, Sage Green. Designed by Captain Robert H Williams, USMC. Early production without the knife pocket on the left cargo pocket for the Western W31 drop knife.

Rear view of 1st Pattern Coverall, Parachutist, HBT, Sage Green. Note the large pocket. When asked what the various pockets were for, Captain Williams replied "I put the pocket on for no particular reason, I figured any self-respecting Marine would find a use for them".

Coverall, Parachutist, HBT, sage green. Detail of large pocket on upper back, thought to have been for the poncho or a general cargo pocket.

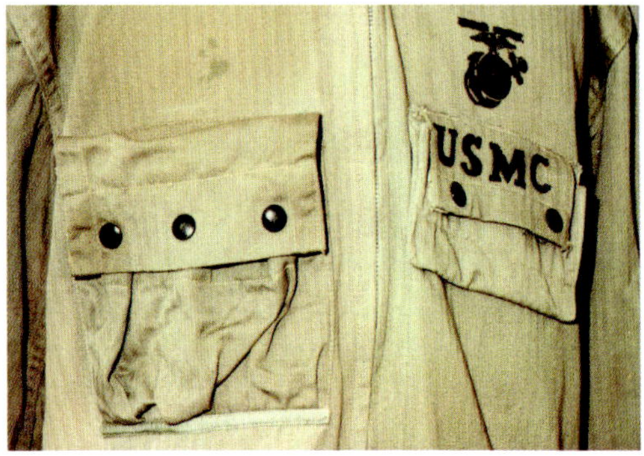

Coverall, Parachutist, HBT, sage green. Detail of upper front pockets, thought to have been for K-rations and first aid dressings.

Coverall, Parachutist (camouflage). Second pattern jump smock, (first pattern camouflage) designed by Lt Col Marcellus J Howard and Capt Harry L Torgerson as part of a 3-piece combat jump suit and intended to be worn over the two-piece uniform, utility, HBT, camouflage (parachutist). Note pocket detail; slanting pointed flaps with three glove snaps on chest and similar flaps across the thighs. Note also front closure by glove snaps and concealed elbow pads.

Coverall, Parachutist (camouflage). Rear view of the second pattern jump smock, (first pattern camouflage) designed by Lt Col Marcellus J Howard and Capt Harry L Torgerson as part of a 3-piece combat jump suit. Note rear 'poacher's pocket' accessed by long, slanting, zipped openings with three-snap flaps. Veterans recollect being told that this pocket was to carry the poncho, but found it impossible to bend or sit down if they tried it. Note also name stencil on inside of right pocket flap.

Paramarine in training at New River, North Carolina, during 1941. He wears the first pattern sage green HBT Parachutist's Coverall over standard one-piece mechanic's coveralls, with high-leg jump boots and the leather US Navy air gunner's helmet adopted by the Paramarines as a jump helmet. Webbing comprises a rifle cartridge belt with canteen and first aid pouch; extra dressings and rations are carried in the left and right breast pockets respectively and the folded poncho in the upper back pocket. His weapon is the Johnson semi-automatic rifle.

Shortly before shipping overseas, this Paramarine training at Camp Elliott, California, wears the two-piece utility uniform, camouflage (parachutist) beneath the coverall, parachutist, camouflage (modified). Note M1C parachutist's steel helmet worn with personally decorated first pattern camouflage cover.

Paramarine, early 1941, wearing 1st pattern jump smock over 1-piece HBT coveralls with 1st pattern jump boots. He wears a leather jump helmet under his M1 steel helmet. Note holster on his right hip for his Reising M55 SMG.

Rear view, Paramarine, early 1941.

Left side view, Paramarine, early 1941. Note lack of knife pocket on left cargo pocket on this early jump smock.

Paramarine c 1943. He wears the newly-designed camouflage jump smock over the new 2-piece camouflage parachute utilities. Note leather jump helmet under his M1 helmet with camouflage cover. Weapon is the newly-issued M1941 Johnson rifle, which replaced the Reising M55 SMG.

Paramarine c 1943 Solomon Islands. He wears the 2-piece camouflage utilities, Parachutist, with 1st pattern jump boots and the M1 helmet with camouflage cover. Weapon is the much-loved M1941 Johnson rifle. Back pack is modified Musette bag.

Close up of pocket details to the front of the 2nd pattern (1st pattern camouflage) jump smock.

Photos of proposed 3-piece camouflage parachute troops uniform submitted by Lt Col Marcellus J Howard and Capt Harry L Torgerson. Photos show 'green side' front and back and 'brown side' back.

Coverall, Parachutist, camouflage (modified). Much simplified 3rd pattern smock (2nd pattern camouflage). Note the 4 pocket snaps flanking the front closure and camouflage cloth covered elbow pads sewn externally.

Coverall, Parachutist, camouflage (modified). Rear view and detail showing simplified 'poacher's pocket', access moved to side seams.

Uniform, Utility, HBT, camouflage (parachutist). Intended to be worn under the second pattern jump smock (first pattern camouflage). The coat is shown here 'brown' side out, note the detail view of distinctive patch pockets, which could be reached through the smock pockets.

Trousers, Utility, HBT, camouflage (parachutist). Detail of front pockets, 'brown' side out, showing bellows construction and three-snap flaps. On the 'green' side the pockets hung internally and there were no flaps over the slash access. (Doug Bailey)

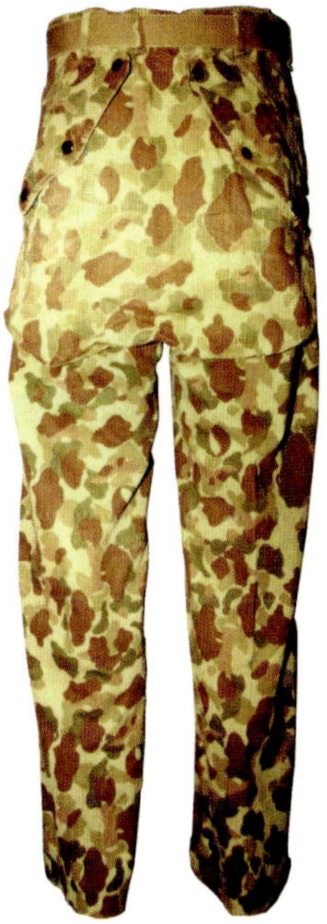

Trousers, Utility, HBT, camouflage (parachutist). Detail of rear, 'green' side out, showing slanting three-snap flaps over access to full-width external 'butt' pocket. On the 'brown' side the pocket hung internally, but access was covered by identical flaps. There were belt loops on both sides. (Doug Bailey)

Paramarine laces up his jump boots ready for a practice drop. Boots are the 2nd pattern USMC jump boots.

Boots, Parachutist – 2nd pattern jump boots made of 'flesh out' leather material, issued from mid-1942.

Boots, Parachutist – 1st pattern leather out boots which could be highly polished when worn with forest green service uniforms.

Boots, Parachutist, USMC – modern reproduction made by Corcoran (makers of WW2 US Army Paratrooper boots), available via WW2 Impressions.

CHAPTER 2

PARACHUTIST HEADWEAR

No. 8788-6
Name Headwear Parachutists
Remarks Front view
JUL 7 - 1941
Copied
Taken

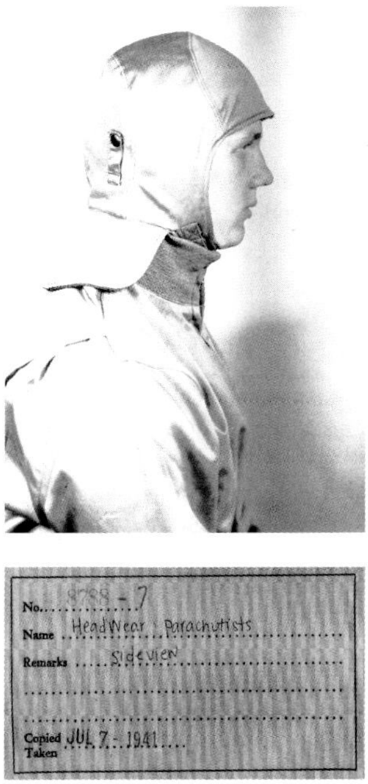
No. 8788-7
Name HeadWear Parachutists
Remarks Sideview
Copied JUL 7 - 1941
Taken

No. 8788-8
Name Headwear, Parachutists
Remarks side view
Copied JUL 7 - 1941
Taken

QM photographs, "Headwear, Parachutist" Basically the Army's Helmet, Combat, Winter dropped in favour of the Navy's leather air gunner's helmet.

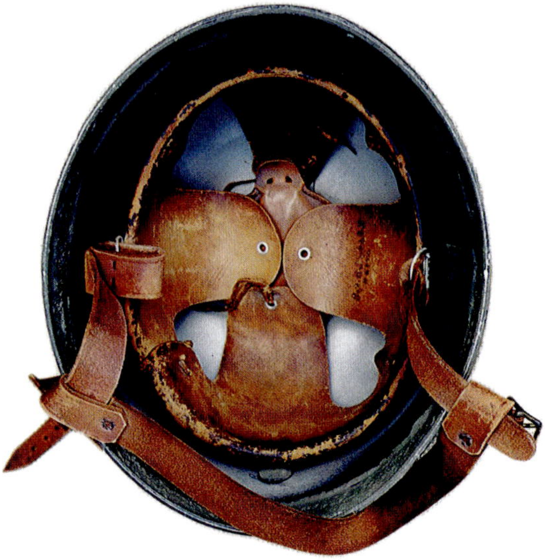

Experimental jump helmet designed at the same time as the 1st pattern jump smock. Note the use of 1917A1 helmet liner. This helmet was rejected as it bore too much of a resemblance to the German Fallschirmjager helmet.

Forest green woollen cloth jump helmet (US Navy foul weather deck helmet) used initially but largely replaced with the leather rear gunner helmet.

1st pattern camouflage helmet cover without buttonholes issued to Paramarines and Raiders.

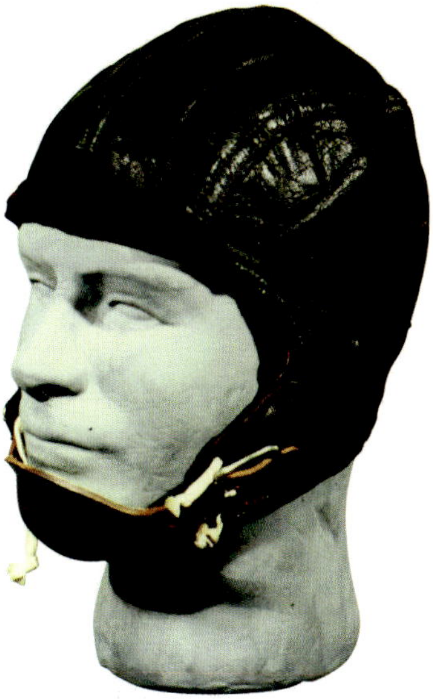

Leather jump helmet 'borrowed' from Navy divebomber rear gunners. This helmet was ideal for Paramarine requirements and was readily available. Note the three-quarter rear loops for securing goggles to the helmet and the four white tapes for adjusting the helmet crown. The leather helmet was worn with or without the M1 steel helmet during jumps. Small numbers of the Army-developed M1C Parachutist steel helmet were also issued to Paramarines, worn with camouflage covers.

M1 helmet worn with leather jump helmet underneath.

M1 helmet camouflage helmet cover, worn over the leather jump helmet.

4th Battalion parachute Marines received the M1C paratrooper helmet, which they wore with the Marine camouflage helmet cover. This was in lieu of the leather jump helmet.

CHAPTER 3

PARAMARINE EQUIPMENT

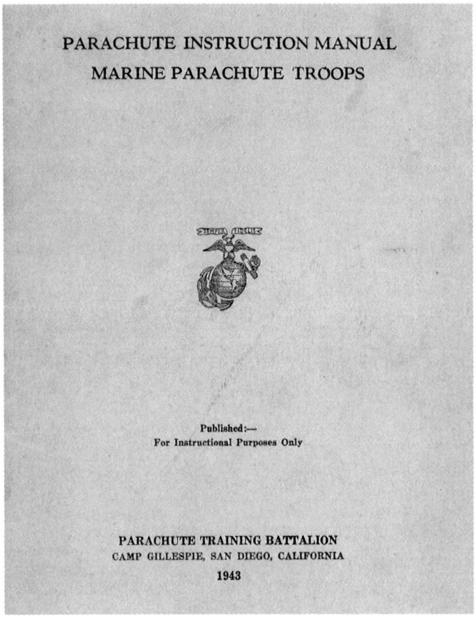

PARACHUTE INSTRUCTION MANUAL
MARINE PARACHUTE TROOPS

Published:—
For Instructional Purposes Only

PARACHUTE TRAINING BATTALION
CAMP GILLESPIE, SAN DIEGO, CALIFORNIA
1943

Parachute Instruction Manual, issued to all trainee Paramarines.

Paramarine just released from Flyaway Tower – Naval Air Station Lakehurst NJ, 1941.

Lakehurst, NJ, 1942. Paramarine (PFC Paul Cook) leaves the transport plane for a practice jump. He carries both main chute and reserve chute.

Paramarine Jump Master checks the reserve chute on a fellow Paramarine prior to practice drop.

Paramarines ready to mount the transport plane for a practice drop. All have Navy TB dual purpose parachutes.

Paramarine makes successful practice drop. Six successful jumps were required to qualify as a Marine Parachutist.

New River, NC. Paramarine floats towards the ground after a perfect practice jump, January 1943.

Lakehurst, NJ – Paramarine practice drop from Flyaway Tower.

Paramarines exit from a Nave R4D transport plane. The Marine Parachute battalions never had enough aircraft for any kind of mass drop during WW2.

Paramarines exit transport plane on a practice drop. Note the method of exiting the plane head first as opposed to the Army method of feet first.

Lakehurst, NJ – Paramarines undergo inspection by a Marine officer Instructor prior to practice drop.

San Diego. Paramarines ready for a practice drop. All wear 1st pattern jump smocks and carry Reising M55 SMGs. Parachutes are Navy TB dual purpose.

Paramarine recovers his parachute after a successful practice drop.

Paramarine Jump Master readies his plane load of Paramarines prior to a practice jump. He is wearing the 1st pattern camlouflage jump suit (designed by Lt Col Marcellus, USMC and Capt Harry Torgerson, USMC)

Paramarine demonstrates the proper method of leaping from a flying plane.

T/Sgt Hal Goodwin, USMCR

T/Sgt Hal Goodwin, USMCR, ready with full gear for a practice drop.

Paramarine ready for his practice jump, complete with main and reserve parachutes and M55 Reising SMG.

A stick of Paramarines board their transport plane ready for a practice drop.

Paramarines exit from a C53 Navy troop transport plane. Paramarines had to complete 6 successful jumps to earn their wings.

Due to the shortage of available transport planes, Paramarines were forced to use Navy blimps for some of their practice jumps.

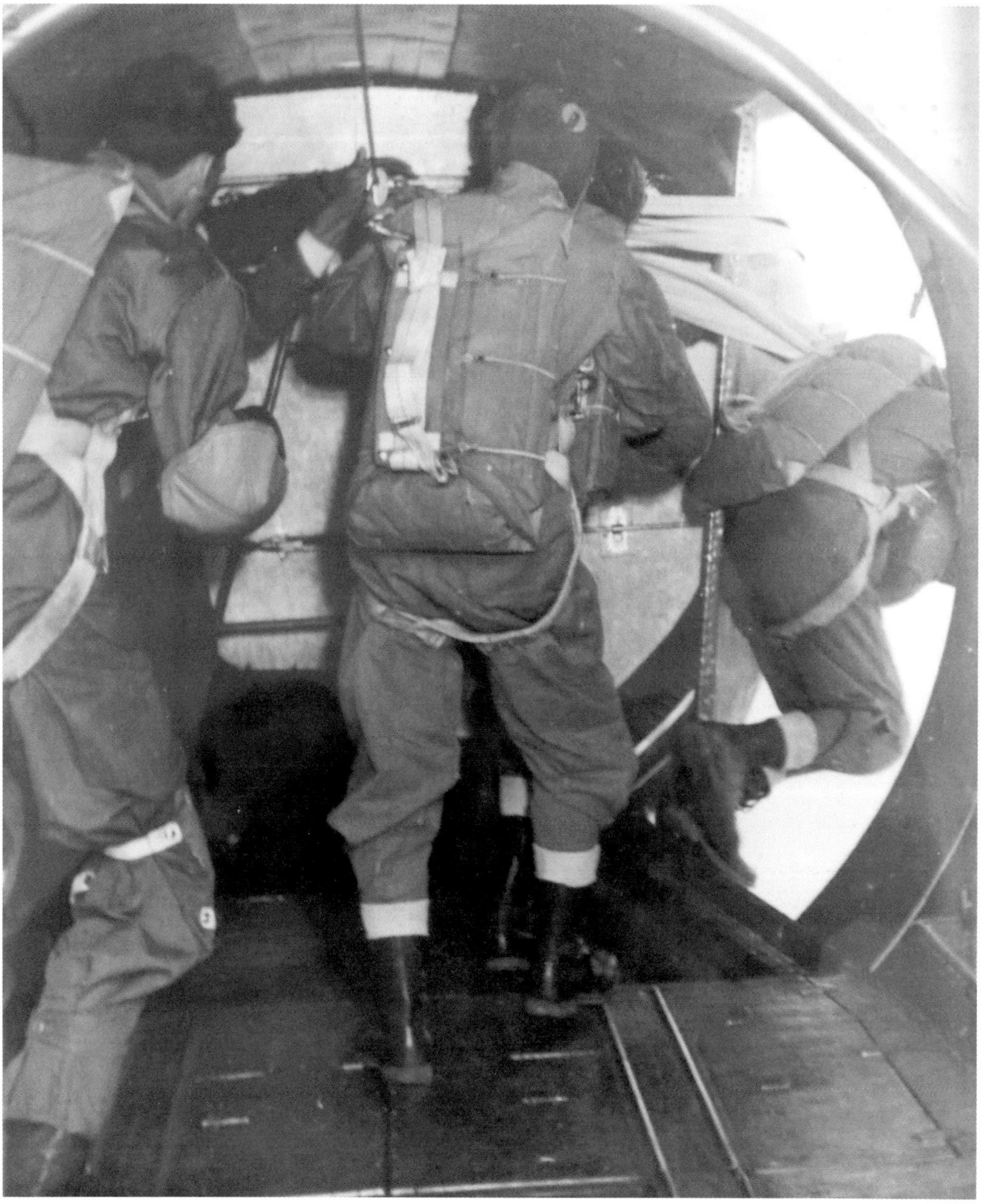

Paramarines exit head first from a Navy transport plane during training.

Fully kitted out Paramarines board a transport plane at NAS Lakehurst, NJ, February 1942.

New River NC, January 1943. Paramarines landing during training. A tumbling technique was used to absorb some of the impact of the landing.

Paramarines give a 'thumbs up' prior to jumping during training at NAS Lakehurst, NJ.

Paramarines receive a final check from their Jump Master prior to loading onto transport planes. Note "K-Bar" knife carried by the Paramarine in the foreground.

Paramarine students descending from free tower at Hightstown, May 1941.

Paramarine student practices a vertical drop in harness at NAS Lakehurst NJ.

NAS Lakehurst, NJ. Paramarine practices free fall from Flyaway Tower.

Paramarine descends from Free Fall Tower, New River NC, January 1943.

Paramarine practising controlled drop from controlled drop tower – NAS Lakehurst NJ.

Paramarines under instruction learn to handle a parachute in strong winds.

Marine glider troops load onto Navy amphibious glider. The glider troop programme was short-lived as there were never enough gliders or transport planes available.

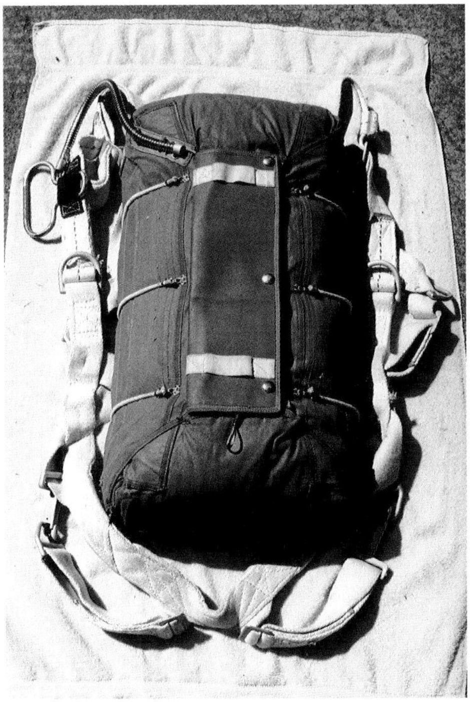

TB dual purpose parachute – main chute.

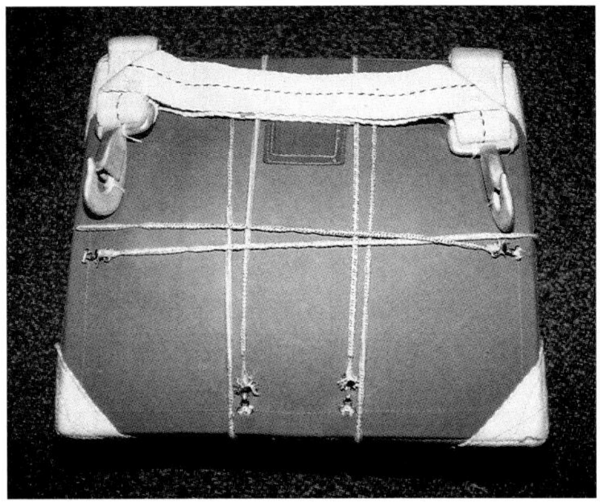

TB dual purpose parachute – reserve chute.

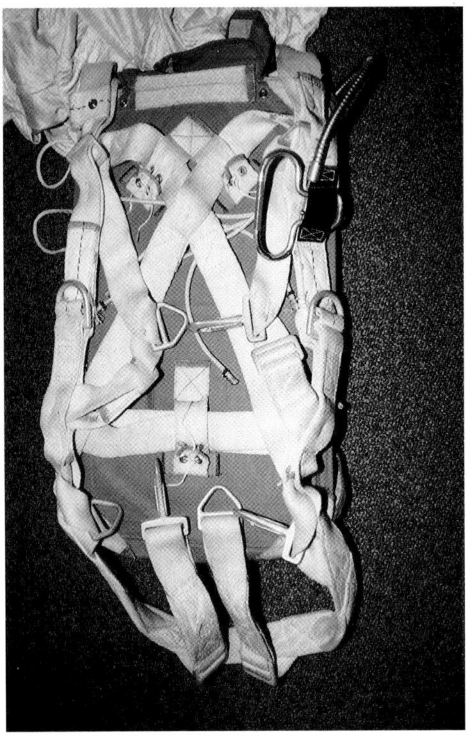

TB dual purpose parachute – main chute.

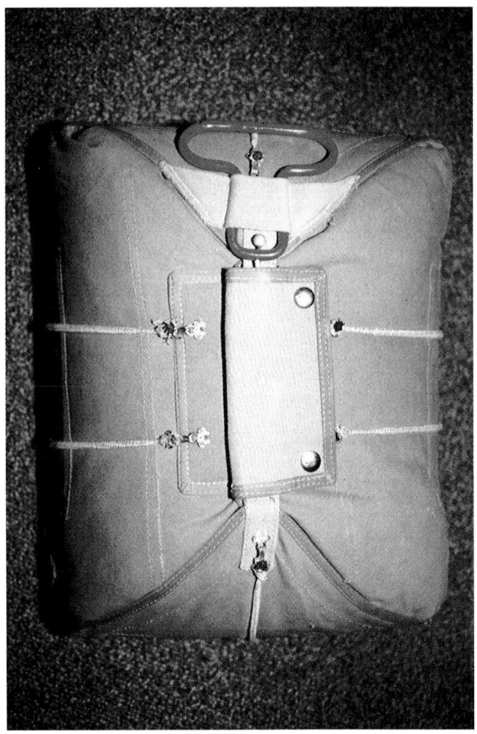

TB dual purpose parachute – reserve chute.

Fanciful image of Paramarines with colour coded parachutes for supply drops; ammunition, medical, rations. This never happened, all Paramarine parachutes were white.

Johnson LMG. Excellent weapon, much loved by Paramarines.

M1941 Johnson rifle. Superb weapon, much loved by Paramarines and intended to replace the Reising SMG which performed badly under combat conditions. The Johnson bayonet proved to be unsuitable and was replaced by the "K-Bar" knife. Unfortunately, issue of Johnson rifles was slow and not all units received them.

Reising M50 SMG issued to Paramarines to replace the Thompson 1928A1 SMG. The Reising did not perform well in combat conditions in Guadalcanal and was intended to be replaced by the Marines with the Johnson M1941 rifle.

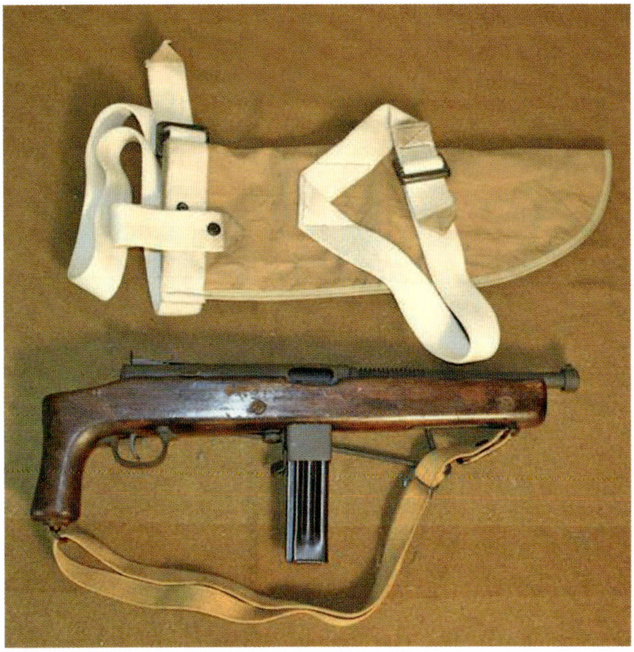

Reising M55, folding wire stock version issued to Paramarines. Seen here with its leg holster.

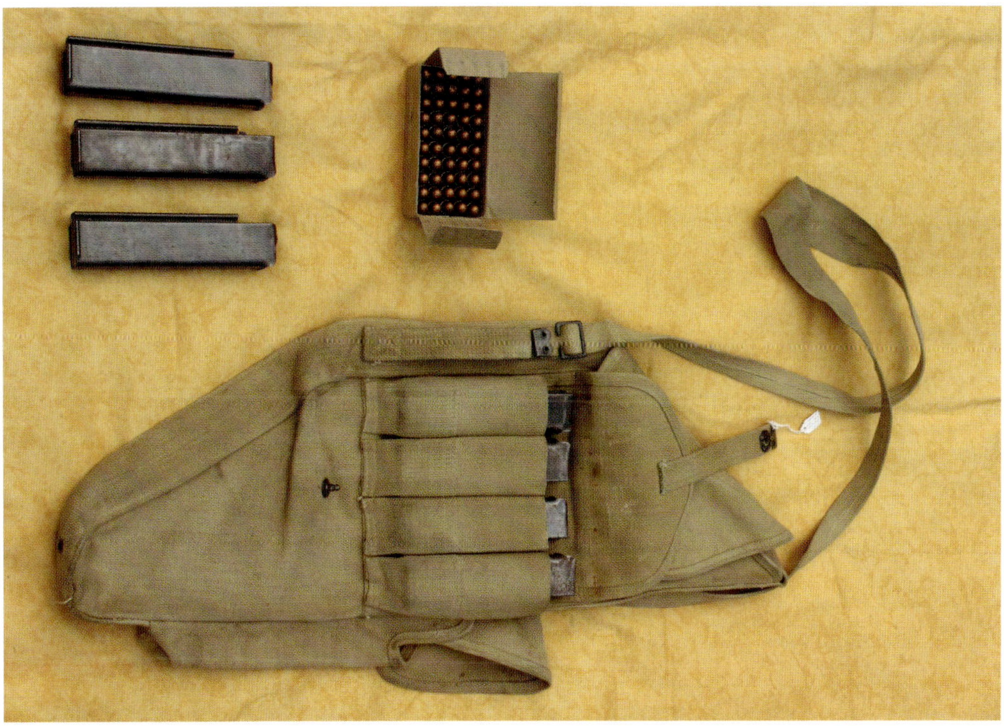

Mounted holster form 1928A1 Thompson SMG. Tried as a means of enabling a Paramarine to jump with his weapon which, in the early days, was the 1928A1 Thompson SMG, but soon to be replaced by the much-hated Reising M55 SMG.

Holster-Reising gun, designed for, and allowing the parachutist to jump with, the M55 Reising SMG.

Drop bag for Reising SMG. Probably rigger made from camouflage material, it could be worn on the pistol belt or on the chest under the reserve chute.

MAB radio, note headphones in skull cap worn under the M1 helmet.

MAB radio worn on the back of a Paramarine. The MAB radio was issued to Paramarine units prior to a parachute drop.

MAB radio carried by a Paramarine. Note headset under M1 helmet, also M1A1 folding stock carbine.

MAB radio issued to Paramarine units. Note tan canvas carry case.

MAB radio in tan canvas carry case. Rigger made carry cases in camouflage material have also been seen.

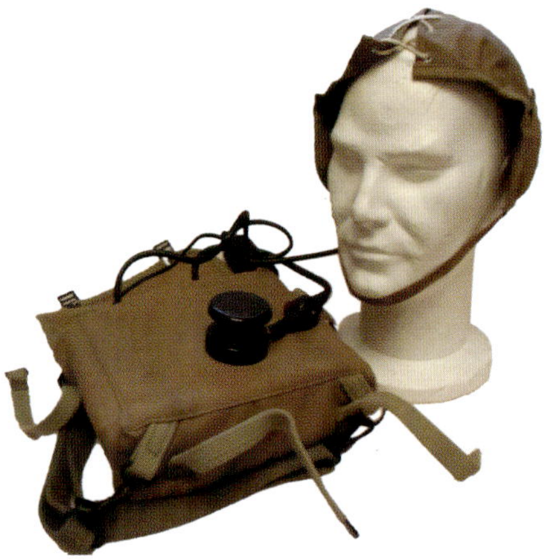

MAB radio – issued to Paramarine units.

Paramarines were also issued with the Raider stiletto, worn here from the cartridge belt.

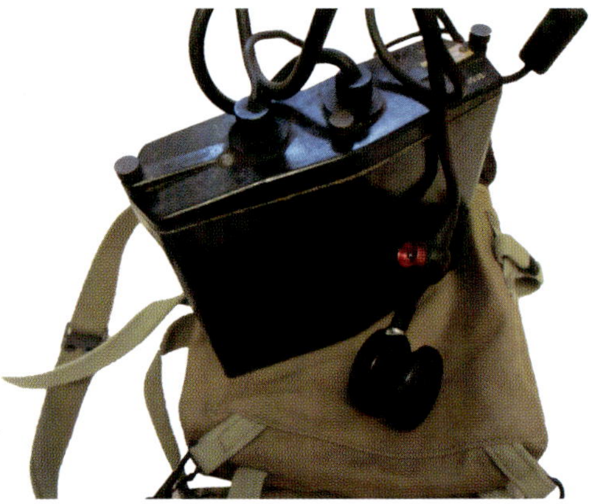

Navy MAB radio issued to Paramarine units.

Raider stiletto – also issued to Paramarines and later replaced by the "K-Bar2 knife.

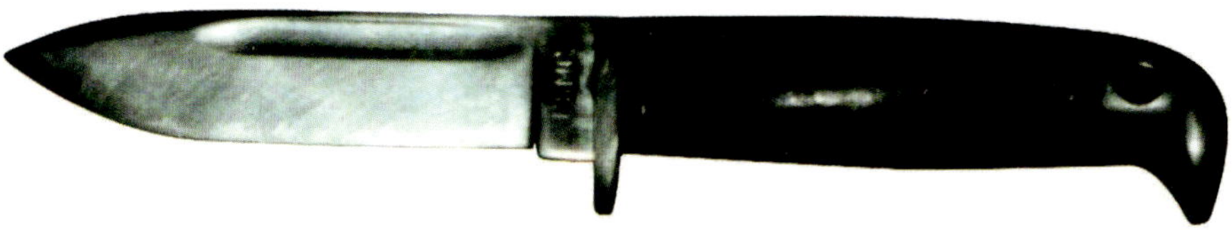

Western W31 paratrooper drop knife. Steel guard and pommel, brown wood grips. Manufactured by Western States Cutlery Co of Boulder, Colorado, for Marine Parachutists, it was intended to be carried in the left external pocket on the 1st pattern jump smock in its small brown leather scabbard. (Doug Bailey)

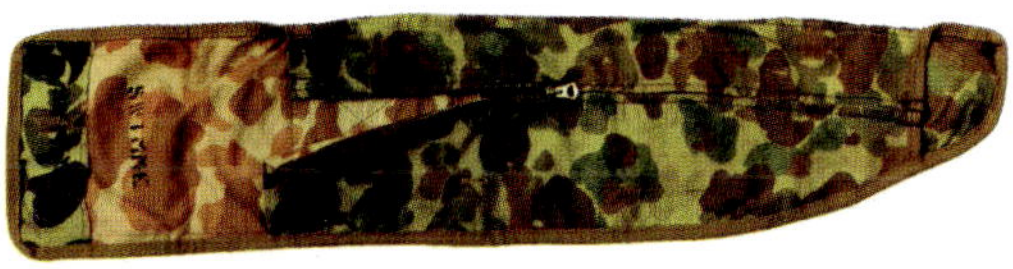

Camouflage leg bag, again designed for the Reising M55 and possibly the M1A1 carbine. This was worn on the webbing belt only – note grommets at the bottom for leg tie; possibly rigger made rather than mass produced (Doug Bailey)

Padded camouflage shovel cover for T-handle entrenching tool. Probably rigger made, the padding was intended to give protection if the shovel was worn on the web belt during the drop. (Doug Bailey)

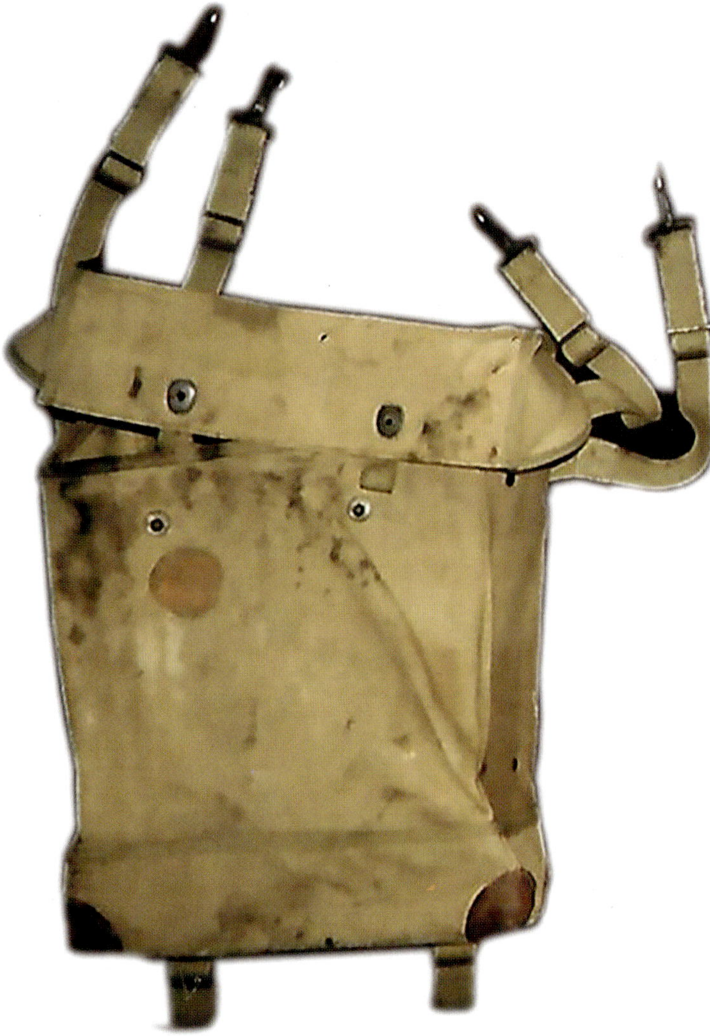

Johnson LMG magazine back pack.

Private purchase knuckleduster trench knife used by Paramarines. Cast aluminium hilt, brown leather scabbard constructed to hang from the belt at an angle. (Doug Bailey)

CHAPTER 4

SERVICE AND DRESS UNIFORMS

Paramarine PFC Robert W Queer home on leave following the Bougainville campaign in February 1944. He wears standard Forest Green winter service uniform, note the gold parachute rigger jump wings on his left breast, also his trouser cuffs tucked into his highly polished jump boots.

Paramarine wearing standard winter service uniform with garrison cap. Note the miniature jump wings on his garrison cap.

Colonel Robert H Williams commanded the 1st Parachute Battalion for much of its early life and led the 1st Battalion into its first combat on Gavutu BSI where Williams was wounded in action. He later returned to the first battalion and would later command the 1st Parachute Regiment. Williams is wearing Officers dress blues, note his silver jump wings.

Paramarine Ira Hayes in enlisted man's service greens. Note miniature jump wings on the garrison cap. Hayes is better known as one of the 6 Marines to raise the Stars and Stripes atop Mount Surabachi during the Iwo Jima campaign. He would later take part in the 7th war bonds tour along with the surviving two flag raisers in Joe Rosenthal's famous photograph.

Paramarine Harlon Block in enlisted man's dress blues, note silver jump wings. Enlisted man's dress blues were not issued during WW2 although enlisted personnel could privately purchase their own. Harlon Block was one of the six Marines in the famous photograph of the raising of the Stars and Stripes on mount Surabachi, Iwo Jima. Block was later killed in action on Iwo Jima.

Paramarine in privately purchased dress blues. Note the silver jump wings, also Marine Amphibious Corps shoulder patch with Parachutist centre. The red backing to the patch is thought to indicate the individual had seen combat.

Silver jump wings were presented to individual Paramarines on completion of 6 successful jumps. It was not uncommon for the individual Paramarine to adorn his wings with a miniature Eagle, Globe and Anchor as in this picture.

Unusual use of Parachutist cuff striker used as an SSI (shoulder sleeve insignia) (Doug Bailey)

Service greens of Paramarine Jack Risler, part of an OSS unit stationed in England. Risler was one of the OSS unit of Paramarines to make a combat drop in southern France. Note OSS jump wings on the right sleeve. (Doug Bailey)

Whilst stationed in England as part of an OSS unit, Bob Lasalle had one of his service greens jackets cut down in the form of an Ike jacket. Lasalle was one of only a handful of Paramarines to make a combat jump (into Southern France). (Doug Bailey)

British paratrooper wings issued to Bob Lasalle whilst undergoing OSS training in England. (Doug Bailey)

Silver jump wings issued to Paramarine Marlin upon successfully completing 6 jumps from a transport plan whilst in training. (Doug Bailey)

Studio portrait of Paramarine Blauvelt in his dress blues. Dress blues were not issued during WW2 but individuals could purchase their own. (Doug Bailey)

Variations of MAC Parachutist SSIs and cuff strikers. (Doug Bailey)

Marine Amphibious Corps SSI with red felt backing, thought to signify combat participation. (Doug Bailey)

Paramarine Blauvelt's dress blues. Note the gilt Paratrooper, Rigger insignia, also Marine Amphibious Corps, Paratrooper patch with red backing. (Doug Bailey)

CHAPTER 5

CHRONOLOGY – PARAMARINES

1940

May — Marine Commandant Maj Gen Holcomb tasks the Division of Plans and Policy with the preparation of a plan for the utilisation of Marine parachute troops. The force would consist of:

- One battalion of infantry at full strength
- One platoon of 75mm Pack Howitzers (2 guns)
- Three units of fire for all arms
- Three days rations and water
- No vehicles other than hand-drawn
- Added light anti-aircraft and anti-tank protection as appropriate

26 October — Initial detachment of 40 trainees (2 Officers and 38 Enlisted) arrive at Naval Air Station Lakenhurst, New Jersey.

1941

23 July — 2nd Parachute Battalion formed, Captain Charles E Shepard Jr commanding with effect from 1 October 1941.

15 August — 1st Parachute Battalion officially organised, Captain Marcellus J Howard commanding

28 September — 1st Parachute Battalion moved from Quantico to New River.

1942

28 March — 1st Parachute Battalion complete.

3 September — 2nd Parachute Battalion at full strength at San Diego.

May — Marine Parachute School Detachment formed. Parachute School, Marine Corps Base, San Diego effective 6 May 1942 and Parachute School, New River, effective 15 June 1942.

7 August — 1st Parachute Battalion take part in the assault on the islands of Gavutu and Tanambogo across the Sealark Channel from Guadalcanal.

8 September — 1st Parachute Battalion join 1st Raider Battalion in Tasimboko raid, Guadalcanal.

13/14 September	1st Parachute Battalion participate in defence of "Bloody Ridge", Guadalcanal.
16 September	3rd Parachute Battalion organised in San Diego under the command of Maj Robert T Vance and assigned to the newly formed 3rd Marine Division.
18 September	1st Parachute Battalion withdraw from Guadalcanal to newly-named Camp Kiser, New Caledonia.
20 October	2nd Parachute Battalion sails from San Diego for New Zealand, arriving 31 October.
31 October to Jan 1943	2nd Parachute Battalion in camp south of Wellington, NZ.

1943

6 January	2nd Parachute Battalion sail to Noumoa, New Caledonia, to join 1st Parachute Battalion at Camp Kiser.
5 & 13 March	3rd Parachute Battalion join 1st and 2nd Battalion at Camp Kiser.
1 April	1st Parachute Regiment activated, Lt Col Robert H Williams appointed Regimental Commander.
2 April	Organisation of 4th Parachute Battalion begins.
September	1st Parachute Regiment transfers to Guadalcanal.
October	2nd Parachute Battalion (Lt Col Victor H Krulak) advised of proposed raid on Choiseul.
27 October	2nd Parachute Battalion land on Choiseul.
3–4 November	2nd Parachute Battalion taken off Choiseul.
22 November	1st Parachute Regiment land at Empress Augusta Bay, Bougainville.
27 November	1st Parachute Regiment designated lead organisation for pending raid on Koiari, Cape Torokina.
29 November	1st Parachute Regiment land on Koiari in the midst of a large Japanese force.
29 November	1st Parachute Regiment task force successfully removed from Koiari.
3 December	1st Parachute Battalion joined by the rest of 1st Parachute Regiment (less 2nd Battalion) on Bougainville.
5 December	1st Parachute Regiment transferred to 3rd Marine Division.
10 December	1st Parachute Regiment relieved by elements of 9th and 21st Marines.
22 December	Elements of 1st Parachute Regiment attached to 2nd Raider Regiment.
30 December	Commandant orders the disbandment of all parachute forces.

1944

2 January	2nd Parachute Battalion moved from Vella Lavella to Guadalcanal.
11 January	Parachute elements relieved by 132nd Infantry Regiment.
15 January	Elements of 1st Parachute Regiment depart Bougainville destined for San Diego.
18 January	2nd Parachute Battalion embark to San Diego.
19 January	4th Parachute Battalion, Col Marcellus J Howard commanding, still in training at Camp Pendleton, is disbanded.
29 February	1st Parachute Regiment, minus air delivery section, assigned to FMF San Diego to form the then-forming 5th Marine Division.

APPENDIX A

COMMANDING OFFICERS, MARINE PARACHUTE TROOPS

1st Parachute Regiment

Lt Col Robert H Williams	1 April 1943–15 Jan 1944
Maj Richard Fagan	16 Jan 1944–29 Feb 1944

1st Parachute Battalion

Capt Marcellus J Howard	15 Aug 1941–1 Oct 1941
Capt (Maj) Robert H Williams	2 Oct 1941–7 Aug 1942
Maj Charles A Miller	8 Aug 1942–17 Sep 1942
Capt Harry L Torgerson	18 Sep 1942–26 Sep 1942
Lt Col Robert H Williams	27 Sep 1942–31 Mar 1943
Maj Brooke H Hatch	1 Apr 1943–27 Apr 1943
Maj Robert C McDonough	28 Apr 1943–9 May 1943
Maj Richard Fagan	10 May 1943–10 Jan 1944
Maj Robert C McDonough	11 Jan 1944–29 Feb 1944

2nd Parachute Battalion

Capt (Maj) Charles E Shepard, Jr	1 Oct 1941–4 May 1942
Maj (Lt Col) Richard W Hayward	5 May 1942–31 Mar 1943
Lt Col Victor H Krulak	1 Apr 1943–7 Nov 1943
Maj Warner T Bigger	8 Nov 1943–29 Feb 1944

3rd Parachute Battalion

Maj Robert T Vance	16 Sep 1942–9 Dec 1943
Maj Harry L Torgerson	10 Dec 1943–29 Feb 1944

4th Parachute Battalion

Lt Col Marcellus J Howard	1 Jul 1943–30 Sep 1943
4Maj Tom M Trotti	1 Oct 1943–19 Jan 1944

APPENDIX B

TABLE OF ORGANISATION (1ST PARACHUTE BATTALION) – 1 JULY 1942

	USMC Off/Enl	**USN Off/Enl**	**Total Off/Enl**
Parachute Bn (T/O D-83)	25/540	3/15	28/555
Headquarters Co (T/O D-82)	10/96	--/---	10/96
Bn Headquarters	9/48	-/----	9/48
Demolition Plt	1/33	-/---	1/33
Co Headquarters	-/115	-/---	-/115
Parachute Co (T/O D-81) (3)	5/148	1/5	6/153
Co Headquarters	2/34	1/5	3/39
Parachute Plt (3)	1/38	1/---	1/38
Plt Headquarters	1/3	-/---	1/3
60mm Mortar Sq	-/5	-/---	-/5
Parachute Sq (3)	-/10	-/---	-/10

APPENDIX C

PARACHUTE BATTALION EQUIPMENT (1ST PARACHUTE BATTALION) – 1 JULY 1942

	HQ Co	Prcht Cos	Total
Gun, machine, .30 caliber Johnson, light	6	81	87
Gun, machine, .45 caliber w/folding stock	106	459	565
Launcher, rocket, AT, M1	---	9	9
Mortar, 60mm	---	9	9
Pistol, .45 caliber	2	---	2
Parachute, set	75	414	489
Truck:			
¼ ton, 4x4	2	3	5
1 ton, 4x4, cargo	1	---	1
2 ½ ton, 6x6, cargo	3	---	3

APPENDIX D

PARACHUTE BATTALION BATTLE HONORS

1st Parachute Regiment

Vella Lavella Occupation	4–16 Oct 1943
Choiseul Island Diversion	28 Oct 1943–4 Nov 1943
Occupation and Defense of Cape Torokina	4–15 Dec 1943

1st Parachute Battalion

Guadalcanal – Tulagi Landings	7–9 Aug 1942
Capture and Defense of Guadalcanal	10 Aug 1943–19 Sep 1942
Vella Lavella Occupation	4–16 Oct 1943
Occupation and Defense of Cape Torokina	23 Nov 1943–15 Dec 1943
Consolidation of Northern Solomons	15 Dec 1943–12 Jan 1944
Presidential Unit Citation	7 Aug 1942–18 Sep 1942

(attached to 1st Marine Division, Solomon Islands)

2nd Parachute Battalion

Vella Lavella Occupation	1 Sep 1943–16 Oct 1943
Choiseul Island Diversion	28 Oct 1943–4 Nov 1943

3rd Parachute Battalion

Vella Lavella Occupation	7 16 Oct 1943
Occupation and Defense of Cape Torokina	4–15 Dec 1943
Consolidation of Northern Solomons	15 Dec 1943–12 Jan 1944

4th Parachute Battalion

None – in training status until disbanded.

RAIDER BATTALIONS

CHAPTER 1

INTRODUCTION – RAIDERS

On 6 January 1942 the first of four Raider Battalions was formed from the 1st Battalion, 5th Marines, and officially designated 1st Separate Battalion. Formed to provide a hard-hitting assault force capable of striking at the enemy almost anywhere and on any available transport, the concept was similar to that of the British Commandos, with whom a group of two officers and twenty enlisted men initially trained in Scotland. On returning to the United States, they became the nucleus of what would become the 1st and 2nd Raider Battalions. These two initial battalions were commanded by officers later to become legendary in Marine Corps history: Lt Col Merritt A Edson and Lt Col Evans F Carlson, respectively. The gallant defence of Bloody Ridge' on Guadalcanal by Edson's Raiders and the daring Makin Raid by Carlson's Raiders were two of the many campaigns to involve the 'elite's elite'.

Raiders were the first Marine units to utilise camouflage clothing, many items being unique to them. Long before purpose made camouflage utilities were made available for general issue, Marine Raiders dyed their khaki shirts and trousers black, as can be seen by the Makin Raid; they sprayed their green utilities and web gear with brown and green paints in camouflage patterns and fashioned their own helmet covers from hessian (burlap) and camouflage netting. The Raiders were said to "carry machine guns like pistols and a knife that was tempered in hell". Two knives, the stiletto and Collins No 18 (so-called Gung Ho knife) were to become forever associated with Raiders.

As the offensive against the Japanese increased in both size and momentum, the specialist role of Raiders (like that of the Paramarines) was no longer considered to be necessary and the four Raider Battalions were re-designated with effect from 1 February 1944 as the re-activated 4th Marine Regiment. The old 4th had been lost with the fall of Corregidor in May 1942. The Marine Raider, like the Paramarines, would not be totally forgotten and indeed their traditions still survive amongst today's scout snipers.

CHAPTER 2

COMBAT UNIFORMS AND EQUIPMENT

Preparing for things to come. The 4th Marine Raiders take a hike at their training base at Camp Pendleton, California. The Leatherneck Raiders are the toughest fighting men in the world. They are selected from the select group of men who compose the Marine Corps. (US Marine Corps official photograph and caption)

A group of Marine raiders, in training at a West Coast base, keep their trigger finger in shape with a little target practice on the improvised rifle range near their camp site. The officers use field glasses to observe the effectiveness of their shooting. Raiders were the first in the Marine Corps to receive the M1 Garand. (Defense Department photograph (Marine Corps))

As sure footed as mountain goats. These United States Marine Raiders dash at full speed along narrow poles. It's part of their training at Camp Pendleton, California. (US Marine Corps Historical Centre)

WWII, a Marine Raider vaulting barb wire. Note newly-issued P42 camouflage dungarees. (US Marine Corps Historical Centre)

Keep it down, MAC! – this ditch with its barb wire ceiling adds point to the warning as the US Marine Raiders at Camp Pendleton, California, learn the axiom of every first class fighting man: 'Keep your rear end down'. (US Marine Corps official photograph and caption)

LCR (Large) being inflated prior to launching.

Over she goes! Quickly the men lower the light rubber boat over the side of the ship after it has been inflated. (US Marine Corps official photograph)

September 1942. Quickly the men lower the light rubber boat over the side of the APT after it has been inflated. Men hurry too once the rubber boat is in the water and equipment is passed down to them. (US Marine Corps official photograph)

Raiders man their rubber boat after successfully launching it over the side of an APT transport.

Recon Marines. Another method of launching the Marine recon teams is to submerge the submarine from under the loaded rubber rafts once the disembarkation point is reached. (US Marine Corps Headquarters)

Start paddling men! In a short time all the boats are over the side and filled with men and equipment ready to practice a landing operation. Each rubber boat carried a squad of men literally armed to the teeth with automatic rifles, machine guns, light mortars, rifles, pistols and knives. (US Marine Corps official photograph and caption)

Raiders practice beach landing from LCR (Large) rubber boat

WWII Marine Raiders manoeuvre in rubber boats (Marine Corps Historical Centre)

Men of the 2nd Raider Battalion arrive back following the Makin Island raid. Note some are wearing their 'black khaki' shirt and trousers.

En route to Tarawa, November 1943: a fine example of the then newly issued 'uniform, utility, HBT, camouflage', complete with first pattern helmet cover. The first pattern two-piece camouflage utilities are worn here with the shirt/jacket tucked into the trousers, 'green' side out, and trousers loose over the field shoes. It is immediately distinguishable from the one-piece Army suit by the pocket details, 'USMC' stencil, and black glove snaps on the trouser fly. (NA 127-N-64176)

Australia, August 1943: PFCs Terry (left) and Freund undergo final tests in unarmed combat at scout/sniper school. Both wear the Army one-piece jungle suits issued to certain Marine units prior to the availability of Marine camouflage suits. Note forest green garrison caps with grommet hole for EGA, also trouser belt used for the machete scabbard. (NA 127-N-60705)

1st Marine Raiders training at Camp Allard, New Caledonia, March 1943: an excellent view of the camouflage utilities first issued to Raider units – note trousers typically tucked into socks. They carry M1 Garand rifles or Reising M55 sub-machine guns; and note men (first and second right) with inner front suspender straps fastened together across their chests instead of to the belt. (NA 127-N-55234)

Bougainville, November 1943: Pte. Bressler, 2nd Raider Battalion, displays a Japanese officer's sword. Note much faded appearance of camouflage utilities compared to those in opposite photograph; and the fact that trouser legs came in one size – too long ... His right leg shows evidence of retailoring with a K-Bar, a common expedient. Horizontal diamond stencils on crates indicate 1st Marine Division, and enclose a unit code number. (NA 127-GW-1060- 69408)

May 1943. American Occupation of Russell Islands, February 1943 – the strategic Russell Islands, 30 miles north-west of Guadalcanal, was occupied by American forces late in February without any Japanese opposition, the Navy announced May 4 1943. Marine Raiders hit the beach and crept cautiously through the jungle. Several well-camouflaged figures advanced through the trees, while others haul their rubber landing boats to cover. (US Marine Corps Historical Centre)

Marine Raiders (left to right) Pte. Fogelson, PFC Kish and PFC Gootee display trophies captured during the fight at Tulagi, Solomon Islands, in August 1942. The camouflage utilities were initially the much prized trademark of the Raiders. Note M50 Reising SMG (left), M1903 Springfield rifle (against tree) and M55 Reising SMG (just visible slung over Goatee's left shoulder). (NA 127-GW-398-55235)

Raider 'black khakis': the first camouflage uniform – for the Makin raid men of the 2nd Raider Battalion dyed one set of khakis black in anticipation of a night attack. They do not seem to have been worn widespread on the raid itself (photographs show the Raiders in two-piece dungarees); however, photographs of the force's return show some of them in their 'black khakis'. This particular shirt was worn by Makin veteran Calvin Inman. (Doug Bailey)

Hand applied camouflage to 41 patt dungaree jacket. Raiders hand applied camouflage paintwork often to their dungarees and webbing prior to the issue of the patt 42 2-piece camouflage dungarees. (Doug Bailey)

Private Roy Grier, 18, of Lumpkin, Georgia, a Marine Raider, is shown here examining a Japanese officer's pistol. Note hand applied camouflage to his dungarees.

Field expedient green and brown paint camouflage on dungarees and webbing: this example was worn on Bougainville by Rudy Rosenquist, 3rd Raider Battalion, and has two missing buttons replaced by Japanese uniform buttons. (Raider Museum)

November 1942, Aola Bay. Raiders' landing operations at Guadalcanal, Solomon Islands. US Navy photograph)

Evans Carlson (third from right) and men of his 2nd Raider Battalion photographed by Ray Bauml shortly after returning to Hawaii from the Makin operation. (via Doug Bailey)

Raider rifle salute to fallen Raiders – Solomon Islands. Note Garand rifles and 2 piece camouflage uniforms.

M1942 suit, one-piece, jungle: this Army-designed item was procured for 1st Marine Division units by Gen. Douglas MacArthur for the Solomons campaign. The rear view shows the 'bi-swing' back. Note also how the suit bunches at the waist due to the internal suspenders – one reason why the suspenders have usually been removed from surviving examples.

Coat, utility, HBT, camouflage P1941: experimental camouflage utility which formed the basis of the P1942 camouflage utilities – note different pocket arrangement, the 'brown' side (left) having only a single left lower pocket; and US Marine Corps buttons in place of glove snaps. The cut is the same as that of the sage green utility jacket. Trousers for the P1941 HBT camouflage utilities were cut on the same lines as the P1941 sage green utilities, having US Marine tack button fly and patch pockets – one front, one rear on green side out and brown side out – which were the forerunner to the P1942 HBT camouflage utilities.

Coat, utility, HBT, camouflage, P1942: initially issued to Raider units and later to scout/snipers, the camouflage utilities were looked upon as a Marine 'trademark', leading to the misconception that 'all Marines wore camouflage and all camouflage was Marine Corps'. The 'green' side of the reversible coat is illustrated; the ground colour was khaki, overprinted with irregular spots of chocolate brown, light redbrown, grass green and yellowish pea green; all shades faded with use and washing.

The 'brown' side of the reversible P1942 camouflage utility coat; note small brown composite button on skirt pocket. The light khaki/beige ground was overprinted with chocolate brown, light drab brown and light red-brown spots, the three-colour pattern giving a paler appearance overall than the 'green' side; with use and washing this side acquired a pinkish cast. Designed for use in beach terrain, the 'brown' camouflage offered little concealment in practice, and its lighter overall appearance was believed by some to be dangerously visible; it is much less often seen in wartime photographs than the 'green' pattern.

Trousers, utility, HBT, camouflage, P1942: first issued during 1942 to Raider units, and highly coveted by them. Unfortunately the glove snap fly did not stand up to field conditions; the single front and rear pockets were also unpopular, many Raiders cutting through to gain simultaneous access to the inner pockets on the 'brown' side.

P42 2-piece camouflage dungarees, issued to 2nd Raider Ben Carson. (Doug Bailey)

Marine of 2nd Raider Battalion, wearing basic P1941 two-piece sage green HBT utility uniform sprayed with field expedient camouflage. The 'boondockers' are worn without leggings, and the trousers are tucked into white 'skivvy' socks. The web pistol belt is supported by US Army M1936 suspenders, preferred by Raiders to USMC issue; attached to it are a canteen, first-aid pouch, Raider stiletto, and 5x20-round Thompson SMG magazine pouch, which also accommodated the magazines for the Reising SMG issued to the Raiders. A pouch for a spare 50-round drum magazine for his Thompson M1928A1 SMG is slung on his left hip. On his chest he wears a World War I eleven-pocket grenade carrier for spare grenades, ammunition and small kit items. The M1 steel helmet has a Raider-made camouflage cover of burlap and string net.

Above and right: Marine of 3rd Raider Battalion operating on Bougainville, November 1943. He wears the newly issued P1942 twopiece reversible camouflage utility uniform, 'green' side out, though showing considerable variation in shades between new and worn items. His first pattern camouflage helmet cover has been personally embellished with the 'bird on a ball' in black paint, unauthorised during the war years. Web equipment is the standard rifle cartridge belt with canteen, first-aid pouch, M1910 bayonet scabbard and 'K-Bar' utility knife, supported by the suspenders from the Model 1941 pack system; note that the gas mask is still carried.

Jungle boots: far superior to the issue boondockers and leggings in Pacific terrain, they were made of green canvas bound with lighter OD tape, with black rubber soles.

Raider boots: Bergmann logger boots adopted by Carlson's 2nd Raiders as an alternative to the boondockers that were standard issue. These sturdy high-leg boots in dark brown leather were superior to the issue boondockers. This pair was issued to Dr. S.L. Stigler, USN, attached to the 2nd Raider Battalion, who received the Navy Cross for his care of casualties on the Makin raid, 17–18 August 1942. (Doug Bailey)

New Georgia, November 1943: PFC Schultz (left) and PFC Harmon compare old and new jungle footwear; Schultz wears the new canvas and rubber jungle boot, Harmon the boondockers and leggings. The jungle boot produced by the US Rubber Company was far superior to the boondockers, requiring only one third of the time to put on and being much more comfortable. An ankle-length version was also produced, popular with Raiders. (NA 127-N-66895)

New Georgia, August 1943: Raiders relax in their jungle camp, wearing the US Rubber Company canvas and rubber jungle boots. (NA 127-GW-1038-61871)

Civilian athletic shoes issued at Jacques Farm training ground to Raider Ben Carson, 2nd Raiders. (Doug Bailey)

The ankle-length jungle shoes, a popular alternative to the jungle boots, also made by the US Rubber Co. in the same materials.

1st pattern tanker's jacket, note Raider SSI (Doug Bailey)

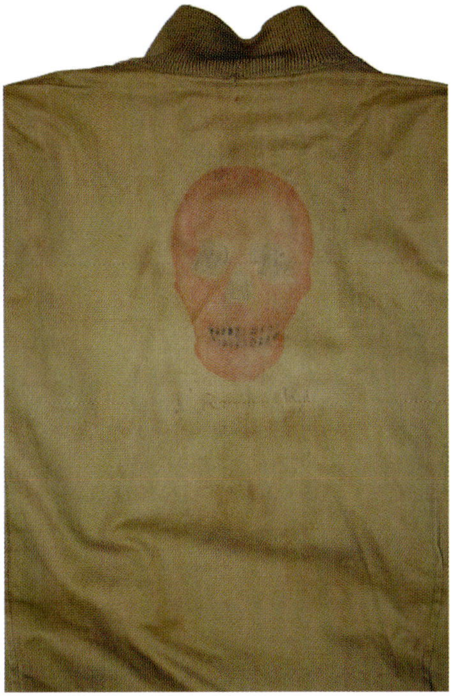

2nd pattern tanker's jacket issued to Raider Cpl Steven Alesich; note Raider adornment on back of jacket. (Doug Bailey)

Jacket, combat, winter or tanker's jacket; these were issued to Raiders, often personalised, as this one. (Doug Bailey)

Raider-made helmet cover of burlap and HBT strips, daubed with OD paint; this example was made by Calvin Inman, 2nd Raider Battalion, and used throughout the war. (Doug Bailey)

Sniper helmet cover, from left side: the integral face/shoulder veil, in a camouflage pattern of black, dark green and red-brown on a pale green ground, was normally worn tucked between the helmet shell and liner out of sight. Unlike the other versions, this cover was of non-reversible cotton printed in the 'green' camouflage pattern only, with a permanently attached green cotton looped band for foliage.

Raiders fashioned their own helmet covers from burlap and netting prior to the issue of purpose made helmet covers. (Doug Bailey)

No two Raider helmet covers were the same. (Doug Bailey)

Some Raiders used their helmet covers through the war as this one, belonging to 2nd Raider Calvin Inman. (Doug Bailey)

Hawley helmet liner belonging to S D Climer, 2nd and 4th Raiders. Note Raider insignia. (Doug Bailey)

First pattern helmet cover of reversible camouflage printed HBT.

Second pattern helmet cover, 'brown' side out: note identifying foliage slits of this type.

Second pattern helmet cover, 'green' side out, from rear: note name stencil.

Sgt. Hensley, 4th Raider Bn., photographed during training in California, 1943, poses with the Western stiletto issued to Raiders before the purpose-made Camillus stiletto became available; the former's blade was believed by some to be too easily broken. (via Doug Bailey)

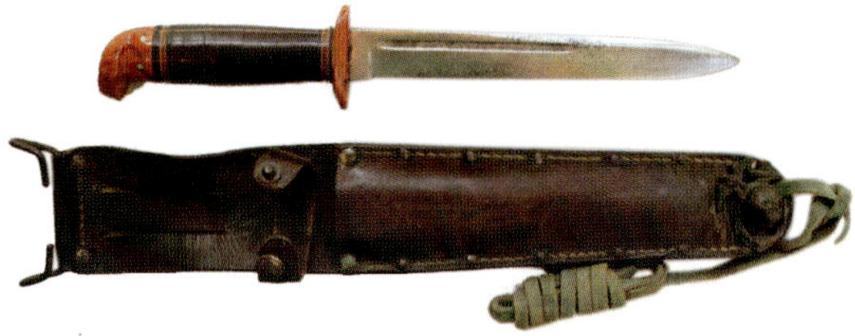

Western stiletto issued to Raiders prior to the issue of the purpose manufactured 'Raider Stiletto'. Note Eagle, Globe and Anchor cap emblem. (Doug Bailey)

August 1942. Marine Corps Raider Battalions, which have participated in the Makin and Solomon Islands attacks, must learn to shoot from any position. This crouching stance, used when running forward, makes a much smaller target than the standing position. Note the knife worn by Marine at left, all Raiders carry them in battle. Note also all are wearing their 'Gung Ho' packs, only used by men of the 2nd Raider Battalion. (US Marine Corps official photograph)

Hunting jacket/pack, acquired by Evans Carlson for his 2nd Raider Battalion. The so-called "Gung Ho" pack seen in use during training but no evidence of its use in combat.

'Gung Ho' knife, No. 456, with green horn grips. (Doug Bailey)

An unissued Collins 'Gung Ho' knife still in its original wrappings; the sheath is plain russet leather. (Raider Museum)

Green horn 'Gung Ho' knife, one of the original 1,000 purchased by Evans Carlson for his 2nd Battalion Raiders. (Doug Bailey)

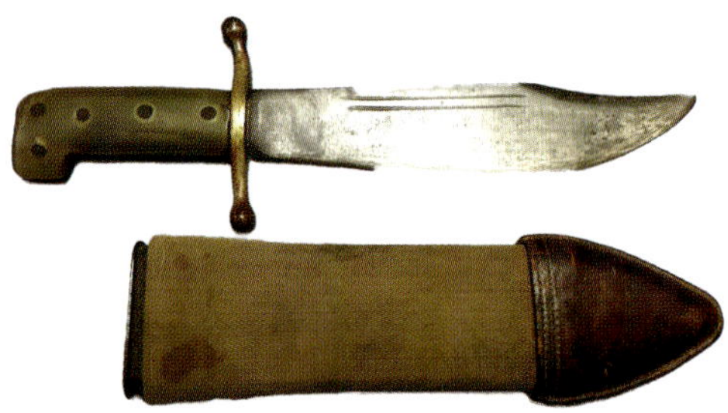

Gung Ho knife, the issued scabbard was very flimsy and was sometimes replaced with a Corpsman's bolo scabbard as here. (Doug Bailey)

Two knives synonymous with the Raiders. Left – Raider stiletto, right – the so-called 'Gung Ho' knife first acquired by Evans Carlson for his 2nd Raider Battalion prior to the issue of the Raider stiletto.

Raider stiletto: of steel throughout, and clearly inspired by the British Commandos' FS fighting knife, this was manufactured exclusively by the Camillus Cutlery Co. of Camillus, New York. Only some 15,000 were made; there were at least three distinct types of leather sheath, the example illustrated being dark brown with brass rivets and throat tabs.

Raider in training, note "Raider Stiletto" on his right hip.

4th Raider in training, note Western Stiletto (Doug Bailey)

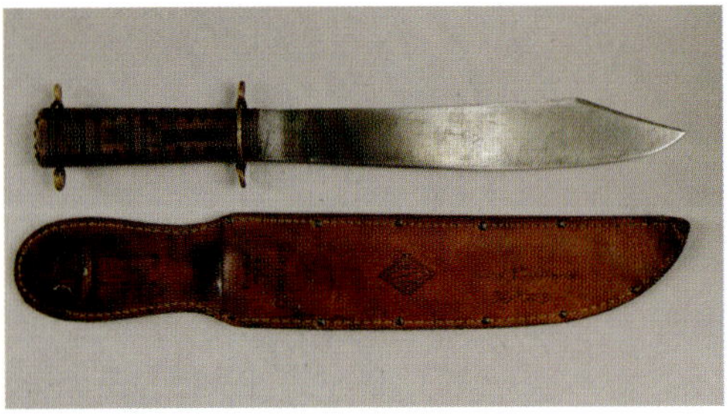

Prior to the issue of the Raider stiletto, many Raiders purchased knives privately, as this owner. (Doug Bailey)

South Pacific, April 1943: Raider 2nd Lt. North sharpens his machete. Note individual-made helmet cover. Raiders were issued a 3-foot square of burlap (hessian) to make their own helmet covers. Note also Raider stiletto hanging from his pistol belt. (NA 127-N-54685A)

Marine issue K-Bar was also issued to Raiders. Note Raider insignia on scabbard. (Doug Bailey)

WWII. Marine raiders crossing the river at Enogai. Note Raider carrying the Boyes Anti-tank Rifle.

Cape Gloucester, 1943: Marine gunners man 75mm pack howitzers. All wear Army one piece camouflage suits and M1936 pattern fatigue hats. Note fire control at extreme right with suit top rolled around waist and legs rolled up. (NA 127-N-71988)

Tarawa, November 1943: Col. David Shoup's command post, showing the mixed use of sage green and camouflage utilities. Shoup is at centre, with M1928 map case, wearing uncovered helmet and plain dungarees. The officer talking to him wears – most unusually, in combat – captain's collar bars. Seated in foreground is the legendary Raider, Evans Carlson, wearing the sniper's helmet cover. Behind him, standing hand on hip, is another Raider legend, Red Mike Edson, formerly CO 1st Raider Battalion. At left, camouflage ponchos are rigged as a shelter. (NA 127-N-63505)

Betio, Tarawa, November 1943: reinforcements prepare to move up to the front. The cameraman (left foreground) wears camouflage utilities 'brown' side out; his uniform – and poncho, also showing the 'brown' side – contrast with the appearance of the other men. Two men (extreme right) carry M2 ammunition vests with 60mm mortar rounds. (NA 127-N-64357)

South-West Pacific, April 1943: Lt. Col. James Roosevelt, 4th Raiders, leads his men back to base after completing jungle reconnaissance. Behind him is Col. Leversedge, 3rd Raiders commander. Roosevelt has a Collins No.18 'Gung Ho' knife on his left hip; and Army M1936 belt suspenders, common in the 2nd Raider Bn. with which Roosevelt served previously. Leversedge wears, as always, a Marine Corps rain hat with cap emblem affixed. (NA 127-GW-494-58311)

Major Evans F Carlson, initial Commander of the 2nd Raider Battalion and instigator of the battle cry – "Gung Ho".

Raiders were first to be issued camouflage uniforms. This Raider has been issued the experimental P41 uniform, the forerunner to the P42 2-piece camouflage uniform. Note the home made helmet cover. Raiders made their own helmet covers prior to the issue of the purpose made camouflage helmet cover.

Tarawa, November 1943: Japanese prisoner being interrogated by 2nd Division commanding officer Merritt 'Red Mike' Edson (second right), former CO of 1st Raider Battalion; note private purchase pistol belt. Evans Carlson, former CO 2nd Raider Battalion (far right) has a slung M1928 map case and a .45 auto pistol worn butt forwards. He also has a sniper's helmet cover. Two Marines in camouflage utilities (far left) are Military Police; left arm brassards are just visible, as is a five-pocket M1 carbine magazine pouch on one pistol belt. (NA 127-N-63788)

2nd Battalion Raiders exercise aboard submarine en route to Makin Island raid.

Raiders undergo training at the 'mud pits'.

Principal method of assault for Raiders was by rubber boat (LCR-L Landing Craft, Rubber – Large)

LCR-L, Landing Craft, Rubber, Large. Mainstay assault craft for the Raiders, although seldom used except during training. Launched from APT transport or submarine (as for the Makin Raid).

Training in the USA, men of the 2nd Raider Battalion wear the civilian manufacture 'shooting jacket/pack' peculiar to this unit, purchased by Evans Carlson; this so-called 'camel pack', which gave the wearer a hump backed appearance, was discarded and thought to have been destroyed before the 2nd Raiders went overseas. The vest type jacket had webbing shoulder and chest straps and an integral rear pack, fastened by cords through grommets. (via Doug Bailey)

Ray Bauml photo of men of Co. A, 2nd Raiders clowning for the camera. They wear a mixture of khakis and dungarees, and the beerdrinker with one foot up on the running board has rubber and canvas athletic shoes, private purchase in black canvas or leather, prior to the production of the military jungle boot and shoe in green canvas and rubber.

Photo taken by Ray Bauml of 2nd Raiders training manoeuvre post Makin raid. On original prints it is possible to make out Raider-made helmet covers, two-piece utilities, 'Gung Ho' knives, M1928A1 Thompson and M55 Reising SMGs, M1 Garands; and World War I webbing grenade vests, as worn in the single portrait of Pte. Alden C. Mattison, killed shortly after he was photographed, on 17 August 1942 during the raid on Makin. (via Doug Bailey)

Camp Catlin, Hawaii, September 1942: Capt. Davis, 2nd Raiders, wearing 'Gung Ho' knife in leather scabbard, and wire-cutters, on his belt. (via Doug Bailey)

Practising hand-to-hand combat, these Raiders both have the Camillus stiletto; note also (right) P1936 musette bag worn as a pack. (via Doug Bailey)

In this snapshot by Calvin Inman, men of Co. B, 3rd Raiders pose with their newly issued 'Gung Ho' knives. (via Doug Bailey)

New Zealand manufactured 'Gung Ho' knife, manufactured at the request of Evans C Carlson, son of Evans F Carlson of 'Carlson's Raiders' fame. These were issued in the summer of 1943 to men of 1st Battalion, 21st Marines. Below is an extract from a letter in 1973 from Evans C Carlson, who served as a platoon leader under his famous father, Evans F Carlson of Carlson's Raiders in WWII.

> *"This is a rough copy of the so-called 'gung ho' knife issued in the (Raider) Battalion, which I had manufactured in New Zealand for personnel of the 1st Bn 21st Marines in the summer of 1943. The blade was made of Australian carbon steel and the handle was die cast of aluminium alloy. The case (scabbard) was made by a manufacturer of sporting goods in Auckland. About 1,000 were produced. Most of these made it through the war or were sent home as souvenirs."*

Boyes anti-tank rifle. .55 cal, manufactured in Canada and issued to all Raider Battalions. (Doug Bailey)

.55 cal Boyes anti-tank rifle 5 round clip. Raiders were issued the Boyes anti-tank rifle or the 'Elephant Gun' as they called it. (Doug Bailey)

Raider in training, still finds time to shave. Note newly-issued M1 Garand rifle and Raider stiletto.

Raider back from the dreaded 'mud pits', part of a Raider's training.

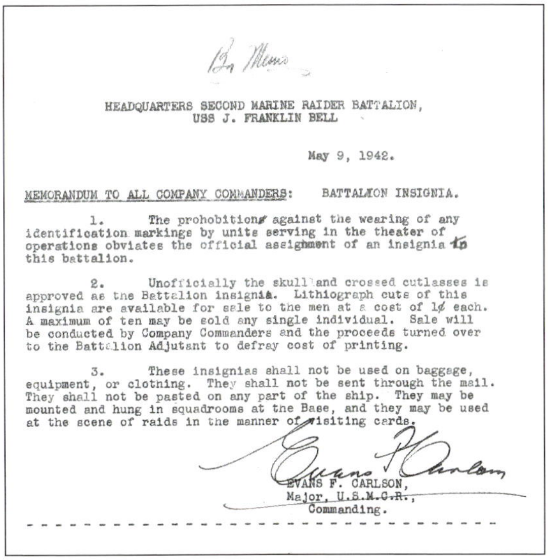

HEADQUARTERS SECOND MARINE RAIDER BATTALION,
USS J. FRANKLIN BELL

May 9, 1942.

MEMORANDUM TO ALL COMPANY COMMANDERS: BATTALION INSIGNIA.

1. The prohobitions against the wearing of any identification markings by units serving in the theater of operations obviates the official assighment of an insignia to this battalion.

2. Unofficially the skull and crossed cutlasses is approved as the Battalion insignia. Lithiograph cuts of this insignia are available for sale to the men at a cost of 1¢ each. A maximum of ten may be sold any single individual. Sale will be conducted by Company Commanders and the proceeds turned over to the Battalion Adjutant to defray cost of printing.

3. These insignias shall not be used on baggage, equipment, or clothing. They shall not be sent through the mail. They shall not be pasted on any part of the ship. They may be mounted and hung in squadrooms at the Base, and they may be used at the scene of raids in the manner of visiting cards.

EVANS F. CARLSON,
Major, U.S.M.C.R.,
Commanding.

Memo from Major Evans F Carlson, Commanding Officer, 2nd Raider Battalion, regarding the use of a Battalion insignia, the so-called "Carlson's Raiders calling card". The crossed cutlasses were later changed to a lightning bolt and Gung Ho knife to be seen on all sorts of 2nd Raider Battalion uniforms and equipment.

Raiders on the rifle range try out their newly-acquired M1 Garand rifles.

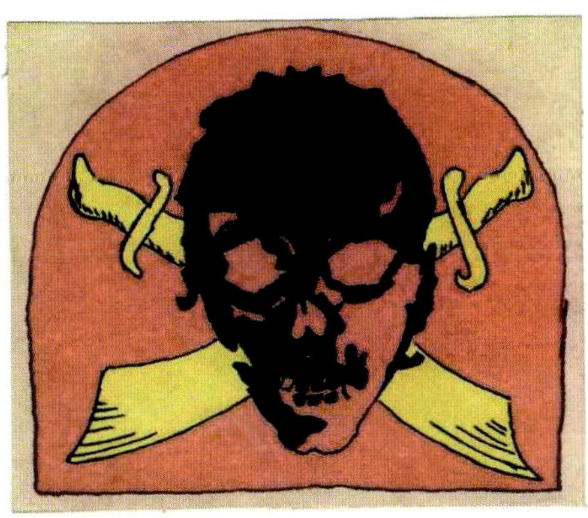

Not strictly 'uniforms and equipment', but a rare piece of Raider memorabilia: 'Carlson's Calling Card', a gum-backed label issued to the 2nd Raiders and intended to be left in prominent places during raids in an early example of this kind of psychological warfare. White label, red panel, black skull and outlines, yellow scimitars.

Canteen cup belonging to 2nd Raider Battalion Raider Frank Cannistraci. Note Raider insignia engraving. (Doug Bailey)

Raider insignia was to be found on all sorts of jackets and even sea bags, as these. (Doug Bailey)

Toggle Rope, issued to Raiders. Useful for scaling walls or trees, also handy to maintain contact with the Raider in front, on night manoeuvres. (Doug Bailey)

War dog. First issued to Raiders for Bougainville operation, November 1943.

CHAPTER 3

SERVICE AND DRESS UNIFORMS

There are many variants of the Raider Patch, both period and post-war. Note 2nd Battalion Carlson's Gung Ho calling card, at left. Also Gung Ho insignia of camouflage pocket. (Doug Bailey)

Service 'greens' jacket issued to Raider Chrest. Note Raider SSI (Doug Bailey)

Close up of PFC Arthur J Gorski, 4th Raider Battalion, service greens. (Doug Bailey)

Close up of Raider Chrest's SSI. There were many variants of the Raider SSI patch. (Doug Bailey)

Cpl George Macrae, 3rd Raiders, in service greens. Note Raider SSI. (Doug Bailey)

CHAPTER 4

CHRONOLOGY – RAIDERS

1941

Summer	US Marine Corps Captains Sam Griffith and Wally Greene observe British Commandos in Scotland.

1942

13 January	Captain James Roosevelt (United States Marine Corps Reserve), President Roosevelt's eldest son, recommends formation of US Marine Commandos. (letter to Marine Commandant). 1st Battalion, 5th Marines is re-designated 1st Separate Battalion USMC.
16 February	1st Separate Battalion is re-designated 1st Raider Battalion. Colonel Merritt Edson commanding.
19 February	2nd Raider Battalion is formed, San Diego. Col Evans Carlson commanding.
7 August	1st Marine Division lands on Guadalcanal, British Solomon Islands. 1st Raider Battalion seizes Tulagi.
17-18 August	2nd Raider Battalion assaults Japanese base on Makin Atoll, Gilbert Islands.
8 September	1st Raider Battalion attacks major Japanese supply point at Tasimboko, Guadalcanal.
12-14 September	1st Raider Battalion repels the Kawaguchi Brigade's attack on the Marine perimeter on Guadalcanal.
4 November to	On the "Long Patrol", 2nd Raider Battalion cover over 150 miles (242 km)
4 December	behind enemy lines

1943

March	1st Raider Regiment formed
5 July	1st Raider Regiment lands on New Georgia
19 July	1st Raider Battalion captures Enogai
20 July	Attempt by 1st and 4th Raider Battalions to capture Bairoko is repulsed

12 September	2nd Marine Raider Regiment (Provisional) organised on New Caledonia
1 November	2nd Raider Regiment lands on Bougainville, attached to the 3rd Marine Division
8-9 November	2nd Raider Battalion in battle of Piva Trail
21-25 November	2nd Raider Battalion in battle of Piva Forks

1944

1 February	The Raiders are disbanded. Veterans form the core of the 4th Marine Regiment (the original 4th Marines were lost with the fall of Corregidor in 1942)

APPENDIX A

UNIT COMMANDING OFFICERS

COMMANDING OFFICERS, MARINE RAIDERS

1st Marine Raider Regiment

Harry B Liversedge	15 March 1943–26 December 1943
Samuel D Puller	27 December 1943–25 January 1944
Alan Shapley	26 January 1944–1 February 1944

2nd Marine Raider Regiment (Provisional)

Alan Shapley	12 September 1943–26 January 1944

1st Marine Raider Battalion

Merrit A Edson	16 February 1942–19 September 1942
Samuel B Griffith II	20 September 1942–26 September 1942
Ira J Irwin	27 September 1942–13 January 1943
Samuel B Griffith II	14 January–8 September 1943
George W Herring	9 September 1943–2 October 1943
Charles L Banks	3 October 1943–1 February 1944

2nd Marine Raider Battalion

Evans F Carlson	19 February 1942–21 March 1943
Alan Shapley	22 March 1943–30 August 1943
Joseph P McCaffery	1 September 1943–1 November 1943
Richard T Washburn	1 November 1943–25 January 1944
Bernard W Green	26 January 1944–31 January 1944

3rd Marine Raider Battalion

Lt Col Harry B Liversedge	20 September 1942–14 March 1943
Lt Col Samuel S Yeaton	15 March 1943–15 June 1943
Lt Col Fred D Beans	16 June 1943–14 January 1944
Maj Ira J Irwin	15 January 1944–31 January 1944

4th Marine Raider Battalion

Maj James Roosevelt	23 October 1942–28 April 1943
Maj James R Clark	29 April 1943–3 May 1943
Lt Col Michael S Currin	4 May 1943–14 September 1943
Maj Robert H Thomas	15 September 1943–1 February 1944

APPENDIX B

UNIT TABLES OF ORGANISATION

Table of Organisation (1st Raider Battalion) – 24 September 1942

	USMC Off/Enl	USN Off/Enl	Total Off/Enl
Raider Bn (T/O D-175)	36/843	2/20	38/863
Headquarters Co (T/O D-174)	9/129	2/10	11/139
Bn Headquarters	7/72	2/10	9/82
Communications Plt	1/22	-/--	1/22
QM and Motor Transport Plt	1/35	-/--	1/35
Weapons Co (T/O D-173)	7/202	-/2	7/204
Co Headquarters	2/29	-/2	2/31
Demolition Plt	2/74	-/--	2/74
60mm Mortar Plt	1/35	-/--	1/35
Machine Gun Plt (2)	1/32	-/--	1/32
Rifle Co (4) (T/O D-172)	5/128	--/2	5/130
Co Headquarters	1/15	--/2	1/17
Weapons Plt	1/29	-/--	1/29
Rifle Plt (3)	1/28	-/--	1/28

APPENDIX C

UNIT TABLES OF EQUIPMENT

Raider Battalion Equipment – 1st Raider Battalion – 24 September 1942

	HQ Co	Wpns Co	Rifle Co (4)
Carbine, .30 caliber, M1	43	62	20
Gun, machine, .30 caliber			
Browning, M1919A4	2	8	2
Gun, submachine, .45 caliber	200	---	---
Mortar, 60mm	4	3	2
Pistol, .45 caliber	2	24	10
Rifle:			
Antitank	4	2	2
Automatic, .30 caliber	22	---	18
M1	89	123	76
M1903, w/telescopic sight	4	---	9
Trailer:			
1-ton, 2-wheel, cargo	1	---	---
1-ton, 2-wheel, water, 300 gal	1	---	---
Truck:			
½ ton, 4x4	12	---	---
1-ton, 4x4, light repair	1	---	---
1-ton, 4x4, reconnaissance	4	---	---
2 ½ ton, 6x6, cargo	2	---	---

APPENDIX D

RAIDER BATTLE HONORS

1st Raider Regiment

New Georgia – Rendova – Vangunu Occupation	5 July 1943–28 August 1943

2nd Raider Regiment

Occupation and Defense of Cape Torokina	1 November 1943–15 December 1943
Consolidation of Northern Solomons	15 December 1943–12 January 1944

1st Raider Battalion

Guadalcanal – Tulagi Landings	7–9 August 1942
Capture and Defense of Guadalcanal	10 August 1942–16 October 1942
New Georgia – Rendova – Vangunu Occupation	5 July 1943–28 August 1943
Presidential Unit Citation	7 August 1942–9 December 1942
(attached to 1st Marine Division) Solomon Islands	

2nd Raider Battalion

Midway	4–6 June 1942
Capture and Defense of Guadalcanal	17–18 August 1942
Occupation and Defense of Cape Torokina	1 November 1943–15 December 1943
Consolidation of Northern Solomons	15 December 1943–12 January 1944
Presidential Unit Citation	7 August 1942–9 December 1942
(attached to 1st Marine Division) Solomon Islands	

BIBLIOGRAPHY

US Marine Corps Uniforms and Equipment in World War II
Jim Moran
Frontline Books (Pen & Sword Books Limited)

Mission Raise Hell, the US Marines on Choiseul October – November 1943
James F Christ
Naval Institute Press, Annapolis, M aryland

Special Marine Corps Units of World War II
Charles L Updegraph, Jr
History and Museums Division, Headquarters, US Marine Corps, Washington DC

Silk Chutes and Hard Fighting, US Marine Corps Parachute Units in World War II
Lieutenant Colonel Jon T Hoffman
History and Museums Division, Headquarters, US Marine Corps, Washington DC

Grunt Gear, USMC Combat Infantry Equipment of World War II
Alec S Tulkoff
R James Bender Publishing, San Jose, California

Johnson Rifles and Machine Guns
Bruce N Canfield
Andrew Mowbray Publishers, Lincoln, Rhode Island

Paramarine, Uniforms and Equipment of Marine Corps Parachute Units in World War II
Chris Mason
Schiffer Military History, Atglen, Pennsylvania

Ortiz, To Live a Man's Life
Laura Homan Lacey, John W Brunner, PhD
Phillips Publications, Williamstown, New Jersey

Our Kind of War, Illustrated Saga of the US Marine Raiders of World War II
R G Rosenquist, Colonel Martin J (Stormy) Sexton USMC (Ret), Robert A Buerlein
The American Historical Foundation, Richmond, Virginia

Dear Reader,

We hope you have enjoyed this book, but why not share your views on social media? You can also follow our pages to see more about our other products: facebook.com/penandswordbooks or follow us on X @penswordbooks

You can also view our products at www.pen-and-sword.co.uk (UK and ROW) or www.penandswordbooks.com (North America).

To keep up to date with our latest releases and online catalogues, please sign up to our newsletter at: www.pen-and-sword.co.uk/newsletter

If you would like a printed catalogue with our latest books, then please email: enquiries@pen-and-sword.co.uk or telephone: 01226 734555 (UK and ROW) or email: uspen-and-sword@casematepublishers.com or telephone: (610) 853-9131 (North America).

We respect your privacy and we will only use personal information to send you information about our products.

Thank you!